DON'T GET THIS WRONG!
WHAT YOU REALLY NEED TO KNOW ABOUT END TIMES

BY **SEBASTIAN LUCIDO**

Unless otherwise indicated, all Scripture quotations are taken from the Holy Bible, *King James Version* (Public Domain).

Periodic Use for Key Word Definition Sources
Unger's Bible Dictionary
Copyright © 1957, 1961, 1966 by
The Moody Bible Institute of Chicago

Vine's Complete Expository Dictionary of
Old and New Testament Words
Copyright © 1985 by Thomas Nelson, Inc.

DON'T GET THIS WRONG!
ISBN 978-0-692-81433-8
Copyright © 2017 by
Sebastian Lucido

Published by
Lucido Media Group LLC
www.lucidomedia.com

Acknowledgements
Jonathan Coussens, Producer
Mary Richardson, Assistant Writer
Chris Shamus (shamusdesign.com), Graphic Designer

Printed in the United States of America. All rights reserved under International Copyright Law. Contents and/or cover may not be reproduced in whole or in part in any form written or digital without the express written consent of the publisher.

DON'T GET THIS WRONG!
WHAT YOU REALLY NEED TO KNOW ABOUT END TIMES

BY **SEBASTIAN LUCIDO**

TABLE OF CONTENTS

SESSION 1: WHY WE STUDY END TIMES — 2
- *Do Not Be Persuaded* — 5
- *Walk in Preparedness* — 6
- *Your First Priority* — 7
- *Endure the Challenge* — 8
- *Change Your Point of View* — 9

SESSION 2: THE BIG PICTURE — 12
- *God's Greatest Masterpiece* — 15
- *God Always Wins* — 16
- *Preserve the Seed* — 17
- *God's Covenant Agreement* — 18
- *How Does God See You?* — 19

SESSION 3: DANIEL'S 70 WEEKS — 22
- *Reconcile the Books* — 26
- *Rebuild the City* — 27
- *Desolation of the Temple* — 28
- *Prophetic Timeline* — 29
- *Timing of the Rapture* — 30

SESSION 4: MATTHEW 24 — 32
- *A True Believer* — 35
- *Believe the Prophecy* — 36
- *Tell Us the Signs* — 37
- *Trapped in Satan's Snare* — 38
- *Holdfast to Your Faith* — 39

SESSION 5: A CHURCH THAT LOOKS LIKE THE WORLD – PART ONE — 42

- *Expose the Truth* 46
- *Strong Delusion* 47
- *Born in Darkness* 48
- *Guard Your Thoughts* 49
- *Narrow is the Path* 50

SESSION 6: A CHURCH THAT LOOKS LIKE THE WORLD – PART TWO — 52

- *The Truth About Love* 56
- *Heed the Word* 57
- *No Gray Area* 58
- *Adulterous Prayers* 59
- *Live for God* 60

SESSION 7: GREAT TRIBULATION — 62

- *The Spirit of Antichrist* 66
- *The Giver of All Things* 67
- *The Seals Are Broken* 68
- *The Two Saints* 69
- *Tomorrow's Headlines* 70

SESSION 8: REVELATION 19: THE KING'S RETURN — 72

- *Look For the Day* 76
- *A Stained Garment* 77
- *The Lion Comes* 78
- *The Salvation Process* 79
- *Fear of the Lord* 80

SESSION 9: THE JUDGMENTS OF GOD — **82**

Request Denied 86
Everyone Goes Somewhere 87
A Harsher Judgment 88
Examine Your Motives 89
Love Is Everything 90

SESSION 10: THE CHURCH, THE FALSE CHURCH AND JUDGMENT — **92**

No Ordinary Day 96
All-In for Jesus 97
Check Your Oil 98
Multiply Your Talents 99
Acquire Or Give? 100

SESSION 11: THE SNARE — **102**

Watch the Fig Tree 105
Tracking Your Steps 106
Cultivate Your Garden 107
Do Not Pursue These Things 108
The Church is Drifting 109

SESSION 12: WHAT'S NEXT? — **112**

The Next Prophetic Event 116
Wealth Is The Motivation 117
The Earth Will Be Shaken 118
Antichrist Breaks Covenant 119
In Our Lifetime 120

SESSION 1
WHY WE STUDY END TIMES

SESSION 1
WHY WE STUDY END TIMES

MATTHEW 24:3-16

³ NOW AS HE SAT ON THE MOUNT OF OLIVES, THE DISCIPLES CAME TO HIM PRIVATELY, SAYING, "TELL US, WHEN WILL THESE THINGS BE? AND WHAT WILL BE THE SIGN OF YOUR COMING, AND OF THE END OF THE AGE?" ⁴ AND JESUS ANSWERED AND SAID TO THEM: "TAKE HEED THAT NO ONE DECEIVES YOU. ⁵ FOR MANY WILL COME IN MY NAME, SAYING, 'I AM THE CHRIST,' AND WILL DECEIVE MANY. ⁶ AND YOU WILL HEAR OF WARS AND RUMORS OF WARS. SEE THAT YOU ARE NOT TROUBLED; FOR ALL THESE THINGS MUST COME TO PASS, BUT THE END IS NOT YET. ⁷ FOR NATION WILL RISE AGAINST NATION, AND KINGDOM AGAINST KINGDOM. AND THERE WILL BE FAMINES, PESTILENCES, AND EARTHQUAKES IN VARIOUS PLACES. ⁸ ALL THESE ARE THE BEGINNING OF SORROWS. ⁹ THEN THEY WILL DELIVER YOU UP TO TRIBULATION AND KILL YOU, AND YOU WILL BE HATED BY ALL NATIONS FOR MY NAME'S SAKE. ¹⁰ AND THEN MANY WILL BE OFFENDED, WILL BETRAY ONE ANOTHER, AND WILL HATE ONE ANOTHER. ¹¹ THEN MANY FALSE PROPHETS WILL RISE UP AND DECEIVE MANY. ¹² AND BECAUSE LAWLESSNESS WILL ABOUND, THE LOVE OF MANY WILL GROW COLD. ¹³ BUT HE WHO ENDURES TO THE END SHALL BE SAVED. ¹⁴ AND THIS GOSPEL OF THE KINGDOM WILL BE PREACHED IN ALL THE WORLD AS A WITNESS TO ALL THE NATIONS, AND THEN THE END WILL COME. ¹⁵ "THEREFORE WHEN YOU SEE THE 'ABOMINATION OF DESOLATION,' SPOKEN OF BY DANIEL THE PROPHET, STANDING IN THE HOLY PLACE" (WHOEVER READS, LET HIM UNDERSTAND), ¹⁶ THEN LET THOSE WHO ARE IN JUDEA FLEE TO THE MOUNTAINS.

---

1. The focus of one generation to another within the church is not to be caught up in _____ things because they are _____. We are to stay focused on the return of the Lord and live like we are going to meet Jesus _____.

2. "End times" is an important subject that should be taught as a regular _____ in the life of a Christian. We are to take what the Lord gives us and pour it into the next generation so they do not get _____ and they keep focused on His return.

3. That day is going to come like a _____ in the night, and if we are not prepared for it we will be _____ by it. But we are children of the light, meaning, we are children of the _____ of the Word of God and we must be prepared for His return.

4. To watch and to be _____ means to continually be alert and ready—not trapped or overcome by the cares of this world. We have a great _____ to teach others so they are prepared as one generation roles out and another generation roles into the faith.

5. God _____ the unbelievers in the great flood, and the same thing will happen with the return of the Lord because Jesus is going to _____ those who do not love Him and do not have faith in Him. Then it will be too late for unbelievers and _____ who are not prepared.

6. If you are spiritually _____ you will understand that many people today have no regard for God and they are _____ from the faith. Even some _____ are going the way of the world and not the way of Scripture.

7. When the apostles asked Jesus for signs of His coming, Jesus told them many will be _____ and there will be wars and rumors of wars, earthquakes, pestilence and famines. These are the beginnings of _____ and we are not to be troubled because these things must come to pass.

8. Christian will experience conflict, pressure, hatred and persecution because of their _____ in Jesus Christ and because they _____ for the Word of God. However, Jesus tells us many will be _____ and hate one another within the Body of Christ.

9. We study end times to _____ our hearts to understand what is coming—because why would our loving God tell us of these things if there was no need for us to prepare? We need to be like _____ and prepare our hearts and the _____ of our children for what is ahead.

10. Our natural abilities and supernatural abilities are _____ that God gives us. God desires us to use our talents to produce _____ in the Body of Christ and in the world. We are to use our gifts to grow in the things of Him and to grow gifts in _____.

KEY WORDS:

(a) Doctrine   (b) Surfeiting   (c) Scoffers   (d) Children of Revelation   (e) Apostasy

_____ Mockery of Christ and His teachings.

_____ Those who have knowledge of the glory of God.

_____ Act of teaching or that which is taught as instructions.

_____ Leaving the faith or disowning the belief in Christ.

_____ Filled with the busyness of the world, drawn away from God.

SESSION ANSWERS:

1. worldly, temporary, anytime
2. curriculum, discouraged
3. thief, overwhelmed, revelation
4. sober, responsibility
5. destroyed, eradicate, Christians
6. sensitive, departing, churches
7. deceived, birth pains
8. faith, stand, offended
9. garrison, Noah, lives
10. talents, fruit, other people

KEY WORD ANSWERS:

c, d, a, e, b

PERSONAL DEVOTION – DAY 1

DO NOT BE PERSUADED

READ: 2 PETER 3:1-14

This week we are studying eschatology which is sometimes referred to as; end times. Not only is our generation called to study and learn eschatology but we are called to teach it to the next generation so they, like us, will also be looking for His return.

Why do you think it is important that we study the return of the Lord?

Why do you think it's important to teach it to others?

In 2 Peter 3, the Apostle Peter is writing to his team and telling them, to take note and remember that in the last days before the return of the Lord there are going to be scoffers who will tell you that things have continued on for generation, after generation. But Peter warns, do not listen to them, do not be persuaded by them, do not buy into what they say. Instead, understand that the same God Who spoke the judgment in the days of Noah is the same God Who spoke the judgment that is yet to come.

Peter tells us that the day of the Lord comes as a thief in the night.

What Peter is saying, is to be ready to meet Christ at any minute or hour of the day.

What does the word *ready* mean to you?

It's a benefit for us to know that the things of this life are temporary and our lives are just one phase of eternity. The smallest phase of eternity! Today, make sure that you are found living in holiness and godliness and becoming prepared, alert and ready.

PERSONAL DEVOTION – DAY 2
WALK IN PREPAREDNESS

READ: 1 THESSALONIANS 5:1-11

You are a child of light. What does that mean? It means we are children of revelation, we are children of understanding, and we know God's Word.

How does a child of light live daily?

Paul goes on to say that we should be sober, in control of our vessel, which is our body; we should be watchful, alert, prepared, and ready. This is a call to all of Christianity that again we live our lives according to His Word.

Paul is telling us that because we have this revelation, we are children of the light, children of the day; we should be expectant of His return, so that when He returns we are not overtaken by the event. We are not to be overtaken by what comes upon the earth prior to His return; instead, we will be completely prepared. We must also be ready to teach this to the next generation.

What does it mean to be expectant of Christ's return?

The return of the Lord is not a time to be fearful, even though the events seem somewhat shaky. As Believers, we are not appointed to God's wrath.

We are supposed to work with God because He gave us His battle plan ahead of time in His Word. God told us what is going to happen beforehand, and the reason why He told us these things is so that we could walk in preparedness and understand what is coming.

It is important for us to continually feed on His Word and revelation because we need to learn about faith and prayer, His Word, and what it tells us to do.

How are you doing this daily?

PERSONAL DEVOTION – DAY 3

YOUR FIRST PRIORITY

READ: LUKE 21:33-36

Like Matthew 24, this chapter of Luke is entirely devoted to the return of the Lord because it tells us the things that will happen before, during and after, His return. Jesus said, "Men's hearts will fail them for fear because everything is going to shake," before He returns. We are also told to take heed and do not allow your heart to be overcharged by the cares of this life.

How can you not be overtaken by the cares of this life?

In Luke 21, Jesus uses the word *surfeiting* which means to have your senses overcharged.

Are there practical things you can do to avoid being overcharged or surfeiting?

Jesus warns of being too busy.

This is a warning to our generation that we cannot allow the busyness of this time to continue to take us away from the things of God.

What are some of the things that take up your time?

Today, I want to challenge you to live for the Lord!

PERSONAL DEVOTION - DAY 4
ENDURE THE CHALLENGE

READ: JOHN 15:17-27 // JOHN 16

Let's be honest, the times ahead are going to get difficult and you're going to be challenged. The Bible clearly states that Christians will be persecuted.

What warning did Jesus give to the Church in, John 15:18-20?

Although life may be hard at times because you are a Christian, be strong. Persecution may not be avoidable, but as Christians we can endure it.

Jesus tells us to be strong throughout John 15 and 16. In doing so, He also gives us hope. Remember that He, too, was hated and viewed as a foolish man.

The good news is; God gave us the game plan and we know what it will be like! It's important to ready our hearts and minds for the future. To remember that as followers of Jesus, we will be persecuted, and that's okay. Persecution for our faith brings God glory.

When the going gets tough, ask yourself:

What am I doing that caused God to take me down this road?

God, what are You trying to accomplish in others around me that they might see You in me?

What should be our attitude toward suffering persecution? Why?

Revelation 6:1-6 outlines the release of Antichrist which is the first seal. John sees a man emerge from the first seal on a white horse, wearing a crown and this implies that he is a political leader, rising to power in peace. The second seal releases global unrest. The third seal contains a man riding a black horse in possession of a set of balances. Then we are told that food will be scarce throughout this time.

It's very important to remember that your circumstances do not dictate God's love for you.

PERSONAL DEVOTION – DAY 5

CHANGE YOUR POINT OF VIEW

READ: ROMANS 8:31-39

While I was going through a very rough challenge a few years back, I remember asking the Lord, "Why is this happening? Why am I going through this?" The Lord spoke to me and said, "Why are you asking Me, 'Why?' If I love you and I have the highest purpose for you, then I see you eternally and I see you blessed. Do not ask Me why, because My motives are always the same. Instead, ask Me, 'What are You doing Lord to position and prepare my heart for what You have planned for me'?"

Looking at trials and tribulations through this point of view changes the dynamics of your circumstances. If you are asking God, "Why?" then in your heart you are blaming God.

Have you ever asked God, "Why?" If so, what was your motivation?

What were some lessons that you learned during those circumstances?

There will be challenging times and circumstances ahead where you may be tempted to ask God, "Why?"

There is a great blessing in heeding the words to be watchful, prepared, alert, and ready.

Nothing can separate us from the love of God. He wants His highest and best for us. It is important to understand that studying eschatology and end times can be a great blessing. In heeding the words of Revelation we can be watchful, prepared, alert, ready, and sober.

How are you preparing your heart?

Take a moment to pray, and ask God how you can overcome the fear of the unknown and also, the fear of sometimes not knowing the reason why.

SESSION 2
THE BIG PICTURE

SESSION 2
THE BIG PICTURE

GENESIS 1:1-16

¹ IN THE BEGINNING GOD CREATED THE HEAVENS AND THE EARTH. ² THE EARTH WAS WITHOUT FORM, AND VOID; AND DARKNESS WAS ON THE FACE OF THE DEEP. AND THE SPIRIT OF GOD WAS HOVERING OVER THE FACE OF THE WATERS. ³ THEN GOD SAID, "LET THERE BE LIGHT"; AND THERE WAS LIGHT. ⁴ AND GOD SAW THE LIGHT, THAT IT WAS GOOD; AND GOD DIVIDED THE LIGHT FROM THE DARKNESS. ⁵ GOD CALLED THE LIGHT DAY, AND THE DARKNESS HE CALLED NIGHT. SO THE EVENING AND THE MORNING WERE THE FIRST DAY. ⁶ THEN GOD SAID, "LET THERE BE A FIRMAMENT IN THE MIDST OF THE WATERS, AND LET IT DIVIDE THE WATERS FROM THE WATERS." ⁷ THUS GOD MADE THE FIRMAMENT, AND DIVIDED THE WATERS WHICH WERE UNDER THE FIRMAMENT FROM THE WATERS WHICH WERE ABOVE THE FIRMAMENT; AND IT WAS SO. ⁸ AND GOD CALLED THE FIRMAMENT HEAVEN. SO THE EVENING AND THE MORNING WERE THE SECOND DAY. ⁹ THEN GOD SAID, "LET THE WATERS UNDER THE HEAVENS BE GATHERED TOGETHER INTO ONE PLACE, AND LET THE DRY LAND APPEAR"; AND IT WAS SO. ¹⁰ AND GOD CALLED THE DRY LAND EARTH, AND THE GATHERING TOGETHER OF THE WATERS HE CALLED SEAS. AND GOD SAW THAT IT WAS GOOD. ¹¹ THEN GOD SAID, "LET THE EARTH BRING FORTH GRASS, THE HERB THAT YIELDS SEED, AND THE FRUIT TREE THAT YIELDS FRUIT ACCORDING TO ITS KIND, WHOSE SEED IS IN ITSELF, ON THE EARTH"; AND IT WAS SO. ¹² AND THE EARTH BROUGHT FORTH GRASS, THE HERB THAT YIELDS SEED ACCORDING TO ITS KIND, AND THE TREE THAT YIELDS FRUIT, WHOSE SEED IS IN ITSELF ACCORDING TO ITS KIND. AND GOD SAW THAT IT WAS GOOD. ¹³ SO THE EVENING AND THE MORNING WERE THE THIRD DAY. ¹⁴ THEN GOD SAID, "LET THERE BE LIGHTS IN THE FIRMAMENT OF THE HEAVENS TO DIVIDE THE DAY FROM THE NIGHT; AND LET THEM BE FOR SIGNS AND SEASONS, AND FOR DAYS AND YEARS; ¹⁵ AND LET THEM BE FOR LIGHTS IN THE FIRMAMENT OF THE HEAVENS TO GIVE LIGHT ON THE EARTH"; AND IT WAS SO. ¹⁶ THEN GOD MADE TWO GREAT LIGHTS: THE GREATER LIGHT TO RULE THE DAY, AND THE LESSER LIGHT TO RULE THE NIGHT. HE MADE THE STARS ALSO.

SESSION 2

1. Humanity lives within the restraints of time because we live by the _____ and by the _____. We live our lives in a section of time but God lives _____ _____. God has no beginning and He has no end.

2. God does not create the earth in Genesis 1. The earth is _____ because there was creation prior to this but it collapsed. There are two theories on this, one is called the _____ _____ and the other is called _____ _____.

3. Satan was already a _____ _____ when he confronted Adam and Eve in the Garden. The gap theory proposes that Satan fell many _____ of years before, and his fall caused the earth to be wrapped in darkness until God turned the lights back on.

4. Satan believes that he does not owe God _____ or that God is his Creator. Satan is very _____ and believes he is self-made. This is the same thinking process of _____ today.

5. God created Satan and God gave him beauty, wealth and _____ but Satan was filled with _____ because of his pride. Satan lost his glory and status when he fell from heaven.

6. Satan was only a _____ of God's light, but God's light lives in Christians today and we _____ His light to the world. God was Satan's source just as God is our source.

7. Adam and Even lived in a perfect _____ and Satan's first attack on humanity was to cause them to _____. It was their sin that placed them in the same _____ condition from God as Satan was.

8. The first lie Satan told mankind is the _____ of how he moves in our culture today. He deceives us into believing there are no _____ to our disobedience and we can live our lives the way we want, with no _____ to God.

9. When Eve eats from the fruit nothing happens; but when Adam eats of it their environment _____ changes. At this point they _____ died and their sin separated them from God.

10. God tells _____ and _____ and _____ that the seed of this woman will bring forth a child (Jesus) and that Satan's seed will bring forth (Antichrist). So now, Satan's new agenda is to find a way to infiltrate the earth by _____ and _____ the seed of the woman.

KEY WORDS:

(a) Gap Theory   (b) Creation   (c) Bara   (d) Young Earth   (e) Tohu

_____ Work of God in bringing into existence all things in the universe.

_____ Heaven and earth were created by God from nothing.

_____ God created a fully functional earth but Satan's fall destroyed it.

_____ God restored and replenished the formless, empty and previously destroyed earth.

_____ Completely covered in darkness and ice with no light.

SESSION ANSWERS:

1. clock, calendar, outside of time
2. restored, gap theory, young earth
3. fallen angel, thousands
4. anything, prideful, humanity
5. status, iniquity
6. reflector, radiate
7. environment, sin, separated
8. foundation, consequences, regard
9. immediately, spiritually
10. Adam, Eve, Satan, destroying, corrupting

KEY WORD ANSWERS:

b, c, a, d, e

PERSONAL DEVOTION – DAY 1

GOD'S GREATEST MASTERPIECE

READ: GENESIS 1:1-3

Have you ever sat and really looked at God's creation? Isn't it amazing? You can see the stars at night shimmering like diamonds or watch the sunrise at dawn as the horizon looks like a blazing orange canvas.

Even as storm clouds cover the sky, with gray clouds and torrents of rainfall, as winds sway the trees; it is a sight to see the wonders of God's artistic hand.

God's creation is amazing. In Genesis, theologians agree there are two theories of how God created the universe. The first is commonly referred to as; The Gap Theory. This theory suggests that between, Genesis 1:1 and Genesis 1:2, there are millions of years. The second theory is known as; Young Earth. This theory suggests that there is a mere six thousand year span between the first two verses of Genesis.

The word "creates" in, Verse 1, is *bara* which means to create something from nothing. Man can reshape, change, and alter things, but only God can create something from nothing.

Then in, Verse 2, it says that the earth was without form and void, and the word used is *tohu* and you will see this word used a couple of times in the story of creation. Tohu means that the earth was essentially one big ball of ice. It was dormant and there was no life here.

Then in, Verse 3, "God said, Let there be light: and there was light." Then, God began to incubate the earth and bring the earth back.

We believe that God sequentially put things together from nothing when He said, "Let there be light…"It was His Word alone that generated creation.

Yet, in all this beautiful scenery there is something greater.

His greatest masterpiece is you and me. We were not an afterthought in His creation. We were the special finishing touch. He longs for the day when He shall gather His children and we shall be with Him for all eternity.

When was the last time you mediated on His creation?

Describe how thinking about creation makes you feel:

How does it make you feel knowing that you were created especially for Him?

SESSION 2

DON'T GET THIS WRONG!

PERSONAL DEVOTION – DAY 2
GOD ALWAYS WINS

READ: ISAIAH 14:12-17

Lucifer was beautiful, anointed, and had the keys to heaven at his fingertips. How and why did something change so audaciously in him? How was his heart so hardened to the things of God?

It was a longing for self-recognition along with his egotism and pride that won in the battle to overtake God. Lucifer defied God by desiring praise and worship like God.

I imagine he was quickly evicted from heaven, tossed out of the Kingdom and forever banished from eternal love, peace, joy, and light.

Now, because of Satan's choice and Adam's fall, we are left with the choice between good and evil every day.

It is only by renewing our mind and submitting to God's wisdom by hearing His voice, that we can overcome the lusts of this life.

What practical ways can you employ every day to rid yourself of all pride and self-arrogance in order for you to trust in God?

What ways does Satan tempt you to trust in yourself?

What ways can you trust in God?

We are ultimately so much greater with God, Who is in us, than Satan, who is in this world. Remember, *GOD* had the authority to cast Satan out of heaven. God won then; God wins now; and God will win in the end!

PERSONAL DEVOTION – DAY 3

PRESERVE THE SEED

READ: GENESIS 6:2-8 // JUDE 6-8

Remember that Satan's goal is to destroy the seed of man, because ultimately the seed of man will destroy him. In the Old Testament, every time you read the term, *Sons of God*; it is referring to angels. In Genesis, we see that the Sons of God are sleeping with the daughters of man.

This may seem somewhat weird to you, and it is weird, but it is in the Bible. It is God's Word.

The Bible goes on to tell us that the seed was corrupted by angelic infiltration in the earth, meaning, daughters and women with angels. This infiltration is part of the reason God destroyed the earth with the flood.

The importance of a righteous seed is put on display with the lineage of Jesus in the Gospels of Matthew and Luke. Even though Joseph was not a participant in the birth of Jesus, in Jewish law, Joseph was righteous. So, that seed traveled through Noah, through Abraham, through David, and all the way to Mary and Joseph.

The main object of the flood was to do away with all this satanic corruption, destroy the giants and preserve the pure seed to make good the guarantee of the coming seed of the woman, as in the plan of God.

Being defeated before the flood did not stop Satan from making a further attempt to prevent the coming of the Redeemer.

Knowing that Jesus was born, crucified and resurrected, as our way for salvation is exciting news! There is now nothing that Satan can do to stop his defeat. We will have the victory and our God will rule and reign forever.

Have you ever thought about these verses in Genesis 6?

How do you feel about Satan's attempt to outsmart God?

Knowing God has a plan from the beginning is exciting.

What are the things that you can see in your life where Satan has tried to destroy you and your faith?

PERSONAL DEVOTION – DAY 4

GOD'S COVENANT AGREEMENT

READ: GENESIS 17

In this portion of Scripture, we see God entering a covenant or an agreement with Abraham.

God created Adam for a covenant relationship with Him. Adam's covenant was a covenant of works, meaning, if Adam obeyed God's law than everything would be great but if he broke the law, he would die. Adam broke God's law so we all died.

But God promised a Savior, a human being sent from the Lord, Who would destroy Satan (Genesis 3:15), thus undoing all that Satan had engineered.

Another covenant God established was between Himself and a man named Abram. God promised him a land, a seed, and a blessing, forever.

The seed was both physical and spiritual, meaning, there would be millions of descendants. Some will be only physical descendants while others will be physical and spiritual descendants of Abraham.

In Genesis 17, Abraham signed the covenant with the act of circumcision. This was an appropriate sign, since God was pledging Himself to a family tree. It was here in Scripture that God created a new type of people, the Jews. God's plan was to use these people to represent Him in the world and to the world.

The covenant between Abraham and God shows God's saving plan for the world. Abraham was a Gentile and God promised to use him to bring the blessing to every family of the earth.

In doing so, God bound Himself to the offspring of Abraham both physically and spiritually.

When we looked at creation, we learned that we are created in the image of God, and we have a responsibility to be godly to the world around us. By the time of Abraham, humanity had failed multiple times, but through Abraham and his descendants, God formed a people who would embody God's intention for humanity.

They would have a relationship with God and demonstrate His power to the world.

With God's covenant promise to make a great nation out of Abraham and to bless all the nations because of him, God was once again reaching out to humanity with His undeniable grace and plan for salvation.

What does God's covenant with Abraham mean to you?

How does God's foresight to bring about Jesus speak to you of His faithfulness?

Where can you see God's plan at work in your own life? In what ways has God blessed you so that you can bless others? How does Abraham's faith affect the way you think about and relate to God?

PERSONAL DEVOTION – DAY 5

HOW DOES GOD SEE YOU?

READ: MATTHEW 11

John the Baptist was the greatest man born of a woman. However, when people would go to see John the Baptist they would see a man, shabbily dressed, with an untrimmed beard. He wasn't the kind of guy who wore Brooks Brothers® or drove a nice car. However, Jesus proclaimed that this man was the greatest.

God sees us differently than we see each other and ourselves. He has a different grading system. He looks at our hearts and the amount of love we have for Him.

Have you ever graded yourself in comparison to others? Is this the way God sees you?

If God were to rate you right now, what are some positive things He would say? And some negative things?

John's life is an example to us of the seriousness with which we are to approach the Christian life. We pattern our lives after John's by first examining ourselves to be sure we are truly in the faith.

Like John, we are to know and believe that, "…to live is Christ and to die is gain" (Philippians 1:21). Knowing this, we can be fearless in the face of persecution and death. John lived his life to introduce others to Jesus Christ, and he knew the importance of repenting of one's sins in order to live a holy and righteous life.

John shows us how to stand firm in our faith no matter what the circumstances. Paul reminded Timothy that, "…everyone who wants to live a godly life in Christ Jesus will be persecuted" (2 Timothy 3:12). But for many of us who live in freedom, persecution takes on a very mild form. As he lived in an occupied country, John had to be aware that anything contrary to utter devotion to the king or emperor was asking for trouble. Yet, his message was unchanging, bold and strong. It was John's belief, his message, and his continual rebuke of King Herod that landed him in prison.

As Christians, we will have our faith put to the test and we will either falter, or like John, cling to Christ and stand firm in our faith to the end.

How can you incorporate some of the lessons of John the Baptist's life into your own life?

How can you best break down the barriers of society and start viewing others like Christ?

SESSION 3

DANIEL'S 70 WEEKS

SESSION 3
DANIEL'S 70 WEEKS

DANIEL 9:21-27

²¹ YES, WHILE I WAS SPEAKING IN PRAYER, THE MAN GABRIEL, WHOM I HAD SEEN IN THE VISION AT THE BEGINNING, BEING CAUSED TO FLY SWIFTLY, REACHED ME ABOUT THE TIME OF THE EVENING OFFERING. ²² AND HE INFORMED ME, AND TALKED WITH ME, AND SAID, "O DANIEL, I HAVE NOW COME FORTH TO GIVE YOU SKILL TO UNDERSTAND. ²³ AT THE BEGINNING OF YOUR SUPPLICATIONS THE COMMAND WENT OUT, AND I HAVE COME TO TELL YOU, FOR YOU ARE GREATLY BELOVED; THEREFORE CONSIDER THE MATTER, AND UNDERSTAND THE VISION: ²⁴ "SEVENTY WEEKS ARE DETERMINED FOR YOUR PEOPLE AND FOR YOUR HOLY CITY, TO FINISH THE TRANSGRESSION, TO MAKE AN END OF SINS, TO MAKE RECONCILIATION FOR INIQUITY, TO BRING IN EVERLASTING RIGHTEOUSNESS, TO SEAL UP VISION AND PROPHECY, AND TO ANOINT THE MOST HOLY. ²⁵ "KNOW THEREFORE AND UNDERSTAND, THAT FROM THE GOING FORTH OF THE COMMAND TO RESTORE AND BUILD JERUSALEM UNTIL MESSIAH THE PRINCE, THERE SHALL BE SEVEN WEEKS AND SIXTY-TWO WEEKS; THE STREET SHALL BE BUILT AGAIN, AND THE WALL, EVEN IN TROUBLESOME TIMES. ²⁶ "AND AFTER THE SIXTY-TWO WEEKS MESSIAH SHALL BE CUT OFF, BUT NOT FOR HIMSELF; AND THE PEOPLE OF THE PRINCE WHO IS TO COME SHALL DESTROY THE CITY AND THE SANCTUARY. THE END OF IT SHALL BE WITH A FLOOD, AND TILL THE END OF THE WAR DESOLATIONS ARE DETERMINED. ²⁷ THEN HE SHALL CONFIRM A COVENANT WITH MANY FOR ONE WEEK; BUT IN THE MIDDLE OF THE WEEK HE SHALL BRING AN END TO SACRIFICE AND OFFERING. AND ON THE WING OF ABOMINATIONS SHALL BE ONE WHO MAKES DESOLATE, EVEN UNTIL THE CONSUMMATION, WHICH IS DETERMINED, IS POURED OUT ON THE DESOLATE."

---

1. Daniel understood prophecy and knew 70 years were determined for the desolation of Jerusalem. He read the _____ and knew the city would lie in waste for the time _____.

2. The commandment of God was that His people plant _____ and _____ for six years, but on the seventh year the land is to rest. The Jews did not let the land rest for _____ consecutive periods of seven years which is _____ years.

3. God had His way and the _____ were taken out of Jerusalem and held captive in Babylon

while the land rested. Daniel knows the end of the seventy-year exile is near, so he begins to seek the Lord for a _____ Word about the _____.

4. The Lord sent the _____ to tell Daniel there is going to be another 490 years determined upon the people. But at the end of that period God was going to finish the _____ and make an end to sin and bring about everlasting _____.

DANIEL'S 70 WEEKS

| NEHEMIAH STARTS REBUILDING | TEMPLE REBUILT | JESUS CRUCIFIED | END OF ALL THINGS |

49 YEARS (7 WEEKS) — 434 YEARS (62 WEEKS) — 7 YEARS (1 WEEK)

5. The four events studied in Daniel's 70 Weeks are:

    a. Nehemiah starts to rebuild the _____ in Jerusalem.
    b. It takes _____ years or _____ weeks for the Israelites to complete the rebuilding.
    c. Jesus is crucified _____ years or _____ weeks after the Temple is completed.
    d. The _____ is the time between the crucifixion and the End Times.
    e. ____ weeks were completed with the death, burial and resurrection of Jesus Christ.
    f. God has stopped the _____ and we are waiting for the _____ one-week time period.
    g. A _____ is a grouping of ____ consecutive years.

6. At the start of the last week, many _____ will come together and sign an agreement allowing Israel to build a temple. This allows the Jews to then go back to their traditional _____ _____ _____. The key player signing this agreement will be _____.

7. In the middle of this last week, which is _____-_____-___-_____ years into the agreement, Antichrist will break the covenant. He will go into the temple and proclaim himself to be the _____, and this begins what is called _____ _____.

8. Jesus warns us to be prepared because there will be great, _____ deception at this time. We are told that even the _____ in the church will be shaken and moved by the great _____ and _____ of Antichrist, but we are not to believe them.

9. Just before the return of the Lord, there will be one day or longer where the earth is wrapped in complete _____. This is called the _____ _____ _____, where it seems God is making one last attempt to gain the _____ of mankind.

10. The Lord breaks through the darkness and returns as _____ shines out of the east to the west. Jesus will circle the earth in lightening as he _____ on the _____ _____ _____, which will split into two pieces.

11. Can you understand how important it is to have _____-_____ of these events given to us in Scripture? The church is slowly eroding away from _____ on End Times, and only those who _____ these events will have biblical knowledge of what is going to happen.

KEY WORDS:

(a) Abomination   (b) Generation   (c) Sacrificial System   (d) Reconciliation   (e) Antichrist

_____ Signifies people living in a particular age or span of time.

_____ What God accomplished toward sinful man in the death of Jesus Christ.

_____ God opposing power that persecutes the Saints of the Most High.

_____ That which is particularly offensive to the natural inclination of the soul.

_____ A group of offerings used to make atonement for committed sins.

SESSION ANSWERS:

1. Jeremiah, scrolls, prophesied
2. seed time, harvest, 70, 490
3. Jews, prophetic, future
4. Angel Gabriel, transgressions, righteousness

5a. temple
5b. 49, 7
5c. 434, 62
5d. Church Age
5e. 69
5f. clock, last
5g. week, 7

6. nations, ceremony of sacrifices, Antichrist
7. three-and-a-half, Messiah, Great Tribulation
8. supernatural, leaders, signs, wonders
9. darkness, Valley of Decision, hearts
10. lightening, descends, Mount of Olives
11. pre-knowledge, teachings, study

KEY WORD ANSWERS:

b, d, e, a, c

PERSONAL DEVOTION – DAY 1

RECONCILE THE BOOKS

READ: DANIEL 9

One of the most significant prophecies in the Bible is found in Daniel 9:24-27. This is the foundation of Messianic prophecy because it establishes the timing of both the First and Second Comings of the Messiah.

The prophecy is usually referred to as; Daniel's 70 Weeks.

Just as the English word *dozen* can refer to the Number 12, the Hebrew word *shavuim* can refer to seven of anything. In this Scripture from Daniel, it is speaking of years — seventy groups of seven years is a total of 490 years.

The opening words of the prophecy make it clear. "Seventy weeks have been declared for your people and your holy city…" (Daniel 9:24). The focus of the prophecy is the nation of Israel and the city of Jerusalem.

The prophecy begins by stating that six things will be accomplished regarding the Jewish people during a period of 490 years:

- Finish the transgression
- Make an end of sin
- Make atonement for iniquity
- Bring in everlasting righteousness
- Seal up vision and prophecy
- Anoint the most holy place

In other words, it was to bring complete reconciliation to the books and to bring in everlasting peace and to seal up time and anoint the King of kings.

At the end of 490 years there is going to be this great completion and sin is going to end. The wicked will be judged and the righteous will be blessed. Daniel is looking at this and thinking; in 490 years it is going to be over. Essentially, all the corruption in the earth will cease at the end of the 490 year period.

How does knowing the end is near affect your thinking?

Does the *completion of all things* scare you or inspire you? Why?

How can you live each day more prepared, alert and ready, knowing that God has set a stopwatch in motion?

PERSONAL DEVOTION – DAY 2
REBUILD THE CITY

READ: NEHEMIAH 2

Daniel's 70 Weeks lays out God's time clock for the end of all things physically and spiritually. Daniel says all spiritual goals will be accomplished within a special period of 490 years. When did that period begin, and when will it end?

It is when Daniel addresses these questions that he begins to give us clues as to the timing of the First and Second Comings of the Messiah.

The prophecy tells us that the starting point for the 70 Weeks of Years will be, "…the issuing of a decree to restore and rebuild Jerusalem" (Daniel 9:25).

This prophecy was given to Daniel during the time of Israel's exile in Babylon. The approximate date was 538 B.C., shortly before the first Jews were allowed to return to Jerusalem in 536 B.C. under Zerubbabel. Jerusalem was in ruins at this time, having been destroyed by Nebuchadnezzar 70 years earlier.

There are three possible dates of when the timing would begin:

- 538 B.C. — Cyrus, King of Persia, issued a decree to Zerubbabel to rebuild the Temple in Jerusalem (2 Chronicles 36:22-23; Ezra 1:1-3; and Ezra 6:1-5).

- 457 B.C. — Artaxerxes, King of Persia, issued a decree to Ezra authorizing him to reinstitute the Temple services, appoint judges and magistrates, and teach the Law (Ezra 7:11-26).

- 445 B.C. — Artaxerxes issued a decree to Nehemiah to rebuild the walls of Jerusalem (Nehemiah 2:1-8).

The decree issued to Nehemiah, seems to be the most accurate date for the starting of the prophecy, because it is the only one that specifically relates to the rebuilding of Jerusalem.

It is a well known fact, even recorded in the secular encyclopedias, that Nehemiah gave this commandment in 445 B.C. It took almost 50 years to rebuild the city because it was during troubled times, but just like the prophecy said, it was rebuilt.

We will learn in future sessions that Jerusalem is God's timepiece for the world.

PERSONAL DEVOTION – DAY 3

DESOLATION OF THE TEMPLE

READ: DANIEL 9:24-32 // 2 THESSALONIANS 2

Daniel's prophecy states that the 490 years will be divided into three periods; seven weeks (49 years), plus sixty-two weeks (434 years), plus one week (7 years).

Let's look at the timing of these events.

Daniel states in, Verse 26, that at the end of the first two periods (69 weeks or 483 years), the Messiah will be *cut off*. This is a clear reference to the crucifixion.

Let's stop right here and take a historical look at this. You see, when Nehemiah gives the commandment to rebuild the city and the clock starts, then 49 years later the Temple and the city is rebuilt. Then, 434 years later, Jesus is killed.

He then states that both Jerusalem and the Temple will be destroyed.

This last week or the last seven-year period is globally known as; The Tribulation Period. We know from 2 Thessalonians 2 that this "prince who is to come" is Antichrist. The same passage makes it clear that his covenant will enable the Jews to rebuild their Temple.

Both passages, Daniel 9 and 2 Thessalonians 2, establish the fact that in the middle of this 70th week (3-1/2 years into it) this prince who is to come will break his covenant and declare himself to be God. This is the "abomination of desolation."

The Book of Revelation specifies that the Messiah will return to earth 3-1/2 years after this desolation of the Temple takes place.

Now, we have the timing of the two comings of the Messiah. He will come the first time at the end of 483 years, and then, He will be cut off before the Temple is destroyed. He will return the second time at the end of a seven-year period.

PERSONAL DEVOTION – DAY 4

PROPHETIC TIMELINE

SESSION 3

READ: DANIEL 9:24-27 // EPHESIANS 3:4-10

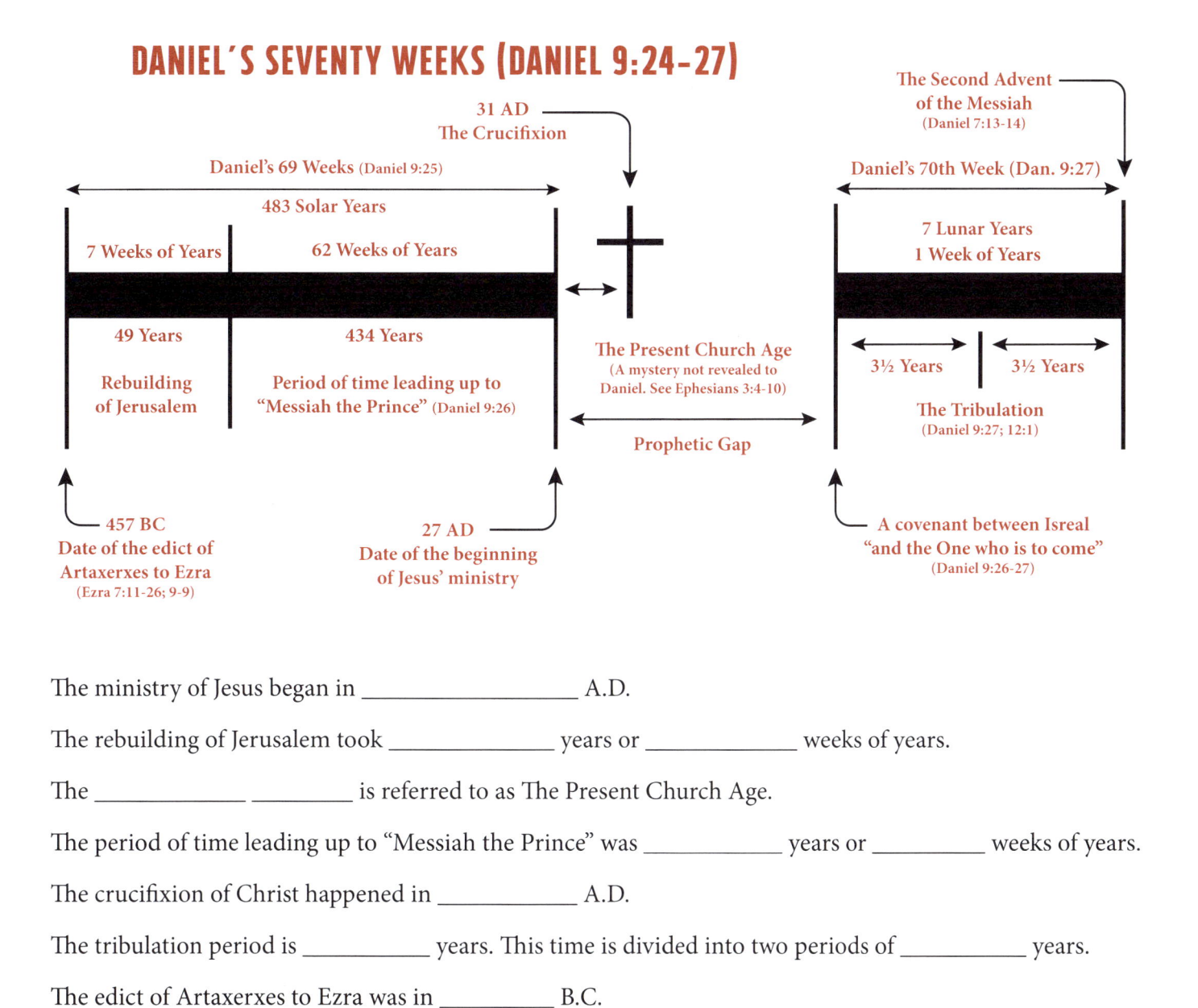

DANIEL'S SEVENTY WEEKS (DANIEL 9:24-27)

31 AD — The Crucifixion

Daniel's 69 Weeks (Daniel 9:25)
483 Solar Years
- 7 Weeks of Years | 62 Weeks of Years
- 49 Years — Rebuilding of Jerusalem
- 434 Years — Period of time leading up to "Messiah the Prince" (Daniel 9:26)

457 BC — Date of the edict of Artaxerxes to Ezra (Ezra 7:11-26; 9-9)

27 AD — Date of the beginning of Jesus' ministry

The Present Church Age (A mystery not revealed to Daniel. See Ephesians 3:4-10)

Prophetic Gap

The Second Advent of the Messiah (Daniel 7:13-14)

Daniel's 70th Week (Dan. 9:27)
7 Lunar Years
1 Week of Years
- 3½ Years | 3½ Years

The Tribulation (Daniel 9:27; 12:1)

A covenant between Isreal "and the One who is to come" (Daniel 9:26-27)

The ministry of Jesus began in _____ A.D.

The rebuilding of Jerusalem took _____ years or _____ weeks of years.

The _____ _____ is referred to as The Present Church Age.

The period of time leading up to "Messiah the Prince" was _____ years or _____ weeks of years.

The crucifixion of Christ happened in _____ A.D.

The tribulation period is _____ years. This time is divided into two periods of _____ years.

The edict of Artaxerxes to Ezra was in _____ B.C.

PERSONAL DEVOTION – DAY 5

TIMING OF THE RAPTURE

READ: 1 THESSALONIANS 4

The rapture of the Church is an event that everyone believes is going to happen, except everyone has a hard time agreeing when it will happen. Some people believe in what is called pre-tribulation rapture, meaning, it happens before the seven-year tribulation period starts. Other people believe that the rapture occurs at mid-tribulation which is at the three and a half year mark. Still, there are others who believe the rapture happens at pre-wrath, where there is a defined period in great tribulation when the wrath of God Himself is poured out on the earth. This occurs between the sixth and the seventh seal because the seventh seal starts the seven trumpets and after that starts the wrath of God. And finally, the last belief is the post-tribulation rapture, meaning exactly that, the rapture happens at the very end of the tribulation period.

These are all pieces of a puzzle that we have not yet lived through but here is the important difference; those who believe in pre-tribulation or mid-tribulation, think we will be raptured while we are living in great peace.

If the rapture occurs at pre-tribulation before Antichrist is empowered then you will not have to go through any of the seven seals or the seven trumpets or the seven vials or experience martyrdom. You will not have to go through any of this because you escape it all. And, if the rapture is mid-tribulation you also escape it all, for the most part, because the first half is peace. However, if the rapture is pre-wrath or post-tribulation you will have to go through lots of turmoil in the earth.

The big difference is; What will I have to do in order to prepare myself and my family? What can I do in order to be prepared to go through this?

These are important questions because if you are the generation that is here on earth, and you have to go through tribulation and you are not prepared for it, well; let me tell you, it is not easy to prepare for a hurricane in the middle of the hurricane! For example, how can you board up your windows and storefronts when there are 140 mph winds blowing? You cannot prepare for things in the middle of the storm; you have to prepare for things before the storm, right? Saints, it is vital that we prepare ourselves and our families!

Those that believe in pre-wrath or post-tribulation realize that we will go through a lot of anguish on earth and so this group must prepare their hearts and minds for tribulation.

Which theory of the rapture do you subscribe to and why?

What happens if you're wrong?

SESSION 4

MATTHEW 24

SESSION 4
MATTHEW 24

MATTHEW 24:1-14

¹ THEN JESUS WENT OUT AND DEPARTED FROM THE TEMPLE, AND HIS DISCIPLES CAME UP TO SHOW HIM THE BUILDINGS OF THE TEMPLE. ² AND JESUS SAID TO THEM, "DO YOU NOT SEE ALL THESE THINGS? ASSUREDLY, I SAY TO YOU, NOT ONE STONE SHALL BE LEFT HERE UPON ANOTHER, THAT SHALL NOT BE THROWN DOWN." ³ NOW AS HE SAT ON THE MOUNT OF OLIVES, THE DISCIPLES CAME TO HIM PRIVATELY, SAYING, "TELL US, WHEN WILL THESE THINGS BE? AND WHAT WILL BE THE SIGN OF YOUR COMING, AND OF THE END OF THE AGE?" ⁴ AND JESUS ANSWERED AND SAID TO THEM: "TAKE HEED THAT NO ONE DECEIVES YOU. ⁵ FOR MANY WILL COME IN MY NAME, SAYING, 'I AM THE CHRIST,' AND WILL DECEIVE MANY. ⁶ AND YOU WILL HEAR OF WARS AND RUMORS OF WARS. SEE THAT YOU ARE NOT TROUBLED; FOR ALL THESE THINGS MUST COME TO PASS, BUT THE END IS NOT YET. ⁷ FOR NATION WILL RISE AGAINST NATION, AND KINGDOM AGAINST KINGDOM. AND THERE WILL BE FAMINES, PESTILENCES, AND EARTHQUAKES IN VARIOUS PLACES. ⁸ ALL THESE ARE THE BEGINNING OF SORROWS. ⁹ THEN THEY WILL DELIVER YOU UP TO TRIBULATION AND KILL YOU, AND YOU WILL BE HATED BY ALL NATIONS FOR MY NAME'S SAKE. ¹⁰ AND THEN MANY WILL BE OFFENDED, WILL BETRAY ONE ANOTHER, AND WILL HATE ONE ANOTHER. ¹¹ THEN MANY FALSE PROPHETS WILL RISE UP AND DECEIVE MANY. ¹² AND BECAUSE LAWLESSNESS WILL ABOUND, THE LOVE OF MANY WILL GROW COLD. ¹³ BUT HE WHO ENDURES TO THE END SHALL BE SAVED. ¹⁴ AND THIS GOSPEL OF THE KINGDOM WILL BE PREACHED IN ALL THE WORLD AS A WITNESS TO ALL THE NATIONS, AND THEN THE END WILL COME.

---

1. Jesus told us the signs of end time events will come one upon another. They will _____ and become _____ just before His return. These events are called the beginning of sorrows or _____ _____.

2. World news will report catastrophic earthquakes, _____ pestilence and famine, wars and rumors of wars, but Jesus told _____ these things must take place. We are not to be _____, instead, we are to be _____ and ready to work with God during this time.

3. Agape love is associated with the _____ love of the church. Jesus warns that Believers will be _____, hated and even killed because of His name. These external pressures will cause many to be moved and _____ from their faith.

4. We see great division in the Church today over _____, laws, and things the _____ is imposing upon us. Many will be deceived and the love of many Christians toward each other and _____ will wax cold.

5. During End Times it will become very difficult to stand as a Christian if you don't understand who you are ____ _____. Those who do not have a heart for the Lord will be _____ and swept away by the _____.

6. In Psalm 2, we are told _____ of the earth and _____ of industry, finance, education and media will set themselves against the Lord and His anointed. They aim to disrupt and cast Christians away from _____ because we are not tolerant of those who _____ God and His Word.

7. The Word tells us when _____ is revealed, the church is going to fail under the trauma and pressure, but there will be a _____ of believers and a _____ of faith that will take place before Jesus returns.

8. We cannot _____ the warnings of Jesus. We have to study the events of _____ because there will be great signs and wonders at this time, and we must be able to spiritually _____ what is of God and what is not of God.

9. Upon the return of the Lord, the earth will experience a supernatural _____ then _____ will shine from the east to the west and His return will be extremely evident _____.

10. The sequence of _____ _____ events will be global upheaval, turmoil and _____ of the Church, great tribulation, then Jesus returns and the _____ of the _____ will occur.

11. There are many _____ who are taken captive by Satan's doctrine. Because of his _____ they are not aware of being caught in his snare. But through love and patience we must teach and show them the way out from his _____ and deception.

12. The church is melting away and morphing into the _____ by not adhering to the Word of God. The body of Christ is becoming _____ _____ and will not be able to stand for Jesus under the _____ that is coming.

KEY WORDS:

(a) Wax Cold   (b) Revival   (c) Deception   (d) Offended   (e) Remnant

_____ Contrast between Church-goers and those who are saved through the Gospel.

_____ False impression given by appearances, teachings or influences.

_____ Cooling off period or a breakdown in the relationship between Christians and God.

_____ Spiritual re-awakening from a state of dormancy in the life of a Believer.

_____ Resentment typically shown due to a perceived insult.

SESSION ANSWERS:

1. intensify, greater, birth pains
2. global, us, troubled, prepared
3. unconditional, offended, depart
4. doctrine, government, God
5. in Christ, overtaken, circumstances
6. kings, rulers, society, disregard
7. Antichrist, remnant, revival
8. ignore, tribulation, discern
9. darkness, lightening, worldwide
10. end time, apostasy, rapture, church
11. churchgoers, deception, trap
12. world, spiritually dull, persecution

KEY WORD ANSWERS:

e, c, a, b, d

PERSONAL DEVOTION – DAY 1
A TRUE BELIEVER

READ: MATTHEW 24

I want you to know that Jesus is talking to His disciples, His Believers and covenant people, those who truly know Him. The Scripture says, "They are going to deliver you up to be afflicted and they shall kill you and you will be hated of all nations for my name's sake" (Verse 9). Stop and ask yourself; Why am I going to be afflicted? Why I am going to be killed? Why am I going to be hated? It will all be for the name of Christianity.

Have you ever thought about this before?

What would you do faced with this type of pressure?

Name three emotions you feel when thinking about this:

Next, we read that nations of the earth are going to persecute and come against the Christian cause. Most often, when we use the word *Christians* it is in reference to a billion plus people on the face of the earth who attend Church, but we know that all of them are not true Believers.

Describe what it means to be a true Believer:

The nations will align themselves against this cause, these zealots and hardcore narrow-minded people, who have a focus on Jesus and claim He is the only way to heaven. It is because of the pressure, persecution and affliction, that many will be offended. Remember, every time you read the word *many* you can know it means most. Jesus is talking to Believers and saying, "The Church is going to fail under this pressure." He is saying that when this pressure happens the end is near.

List a few things that may be part of this pressure and what you can do to overcome it:

Jesus warns us that many false prophets (teachers, pastors, evangelists or leaders) will arise and deceive many with false doctrine. The love of many will wax cold because of iniquity and the social environment will be energized with sin.

How can you protect yourself against false doctrine?

How will you try to evangelize in an environment energized with sin?

PERSONAL DEVOTION – DAY 2

BELIEVE THE PROPHECY

READ: MATHEW 24:1-14

Even today, the view of Jerusalem at sunset from the Mount of Olives is breathtaking. In the time of Jesus, it was even more beautiful because the Temple was still standing. At sunset, the white limestone exterior of the Temple took on a bright golden hue, as if it were made of pure gold. To those living near or around Jerusalem, it was the most beautiful building imaginable.

Late that afternoon, as the disciples and Jesus climbed the mountain outside the city, the proceeding events had to weigh heavily on their minds. Jesus had prophesied the Temple's destruction, and then, blamed it on the Church leaders.

Can you imagine walking up to your pastor and saying, "Because of you, this place is going to burn!" It's easy to see how Jesus wasn't very popular with the religious leaders.

Imagine this sunset walk. For about fifteen or thirty minutes, the disciples had time to think about what Jesus had said and what it could possibly mean.

According to Mark 13:3, the questions were asked by Peter, James, John, and Andrew. The Gospels of Matthew and Mark say the four came "privately" to Jesus.

Maybe they asked in a whisper, "...Tell us, when will these things be? And what will be the sign of Your coming, and of the end of the age?" (Matthew 24:3).

By their questions, the disciples make it very clear; they saw the destruction of the Temple as a sign of the Lord's Kingdom becoming a reality.

Why would the disciples connect the destruction of the Temple with Christ's return?

They knew about the prophesies from the Old Testament and they knew that the destruction of Jerusalem would usher in the Messiah's Kingdom. And in the day of the Lord, Jerusalem is destroyed and the Lord comes with all His saints. (Zechariah 14:1-5).

The disciples were also familiar with and believed the prophecy of Daniel 9:26. The coming of the Messiah would happen simultaneously with the destruction of Jerusalem and the Temple.

So, maybe the disciples expected a different response. It was very common for Jesus to answer questions in stories or even with other questions, but this time it was different. As the sun set over an ancient Jerusalem, Jesus actually answered their questions. And straightforwardly at that! He then goes on to give examples by referring to Noah.

If you take this particular section in Matthew, just for its real estate, Matthew gives The End of the Age more time in his Gospel than, The Beatitudes, The Lord's Prayer and even The Last Supper.

Why is it then, that the modern Church has not paid more attention to the content and context of Matthew 24?

PERSONAL DEVOTION – DAY 3

TELL US THE SIGNS

READ: MATTHEW 24:15-31

Imagine the jaw dropping news Jesus is delivering to the disciples as He continues to describe sign, after sign, after sign, of the end of the world. I can see them all standing around in shock as Jesus says that when tribulation comes, "Let him which is on the housetop not come down to take anything out of his house" (Verse 17). He is basically saying; don't pack, just RUN! Workers in the field are told not to go back home because it is going to be so quick and so rapid that you won't have time. And, if you live in Judea, around Jerusalem, get out of town and go into the mountains to get away from the city.

At this point, the disciples must have thought the desolation of the Temple in Jerusalem was the "sign" of the end they were looking for. But they were incorrect. Jesus continues His answer by saying, "If anyone says to you, `Look, here is the Christ!' or, `There he is!' do not believe it" (Verse 23).

Put the brakes on! We asked Him when the end is and He keeps talking about when the end is *not*. The falling away, the earthquakes and the destruction of the Temple all look like a sign, but Jesus says, these things are not a sign.

Jesus was driving home the point that His disciples should not be deceived either by world events or by people claiming to know when the "sign of the end" had occurred.

There will be great signs and wonders and you cannot look at miracles, you have to look at the Word. This is how you will stay grounded. The Bible says that Antichrist would be wounded and healed. Now, did God heal this wound for Antichrist? No, of course not! Things will be very, very, deceptive in the end!

In Verse 29, Jesus began telling the disciples about the "sign" of His coming. The sun and moon would be darkened and stars, perhaps comets or meteorites, would fall from the sky. The solar system itself would be shaken.

Finally, Jesus gave the disciples the "sign," which is the answer to their question. He said: "At that time the sign of the Son of Man will appear in the sky, and all the nations of the earth will mourn. They will see the Son of Man coming on the clouds of the sky, with power and great glory" (Verse 30).

He comes as lightening from out of the east to the west. He comes in the clouds. There is an angel and a trumpet, and then, we are gathered together. Do you to see the correlation of His return and the rapture of the Church?

Jesus answered the two questions: What will be the sign of Your coming? And, the end of the age? The answer is; there is global upheaval, then turmoil within the body of Christ, then great tribulation, and then, Jesus returns.

PERSONAL DEVOTION – DAY 4

TRAPPED IN SATAN'S SNARE

READ: 2 TIMOTHY 2:24-26 // 2 TIMOTHY 3

In 2 Timothy 2 and 3, Paul is talking about the Church and Believers. He is saying that those of us who know the truth should not fight with Believers who do not. We should not be angry with them, but with patience we should teach God's ways, so that they would know the truth and repent and recover themselves out of the snare of Satan. (2 Timothy 2:26).

Stop and picture what Paul is saying here, he is saying that there are many, many, Church members in Satan's snare.

Here, we have to understand that Paul is talking about people who are Believer's that have been taken captive by Satan's doctrine and not God's doctrine. Because they are taken captive they do not even know they are in Satan's snare. They have no clue, so they are trapped.

Paul is saying that in the last days the snare of Satan is going to be much more intense than in the time when Paul wrote this letter. The condition of the Church or self-identified Christians is going to look just like the world. It is going to have a form of godliness but it is going to deny the power of the Holy Spirit! (2 Timothy 3:5).

Paul instructs us to look at his doctrine and his manner of life, because it is not of the world. Paul tells us, "Listen, if I was self-centered, I would have never gone into Lystra!" When you have a Church that is melting away and morphing into the world and not adhering to the Word of God, then you have a Church that is spiritually dull and cannot stand under the persecution that is coming!

What then is good for doctrine? The starting point of a Christian is to know that God can write a book; the Bible, and He is the same God that created the sun and the moon, the stars and the universe.

God wrote the Bible and His Word is profitable for our doctrine, and it is profitable to instruct and correct us, because it is the Word of God that sets the standard and changes us. We cannot get it right on our own because man left to himself will not find God or the will of God! This is why we look to the Scriptures to teach us doctrine, to correct us, and to instruct us.

This is why it's important to read the Bible every day. It's the divider of truth. Through the Word of God we can know His will for our lives and have our minds renewed to His way of life.

PERSONAL DEVOTION – DAY 5

HOLDFAST TO YOUR FAITH

READ: 2 TIMOTHY 4

In 2 Timothy 4, we see the Apostle Paul's carefully chosen final words. When he chose his last words to Timothy, he decided to encourage his young follower to persevere and to run the race for Christ without fear.

Paul said, "I have fought the good fight. I have finished the race…" (Verse 7). There is a celebration to look forward to as we get closer to the finish line. Our goal is to run through the finish line with celebration that we completed the race!

The greatest disappointments in life come when you start something, but then you do not finish. Think about this because the experiences that you feel disappointed in are the things you didn't finish or you never even started. For example, maybe it is giving up on your marriage or your education or your career or even holding fast in your faith. Then, the emotions of, 'Why didn't I press ahead? Why did I give up?' can sometimes be overwhelming.

Paul wasn't going to end his life in defeat. While some had fallen away, he could still say, "…I have kept the faith" (Verse 7). He didn't lose it, distort it, or fail to pass it on. He kept it and his faith kept him.

As we studied Matthew 24 this week, it's important to remember that our faith will be tested. The world will persecute those who believe. I wish I could say it will be easy, but I can't. Just like the Apostle Paul, we have to continue on in the faith through trials and tribulation. Keep the faith. Protect the faith. And, pass the faith on.

Paul encourages us that beyond the finish line a great reward awaits those who endure. He had his eyes on the great reward of finishing the race. "Henceforth there is laid up for me the crown of righteousness. The crown of righteousness, which the Lord, the righteous judge, will award to me on that Day, and not only to me but also to all who have loved his appearing" (Verse 8).

Paul describes the persevering Believer as one who "loved his appearing."

He looks to the future, waiting for the day Christ will return, and desiring to be found faithful.

Does that describe you?

Are you fighting the good fight, finishing the race and keeping the faith?

How can you prepare and pass on this information to others, like Paul did with Timothy?

The Day is coming and if you are prepared your crown will be waiting!

SESSION 5

A CHURCH THAT LOOKS LIKE THE WORLD – PART ONE

SESSION 5

A CHURCH THAT LOOKS LIKE THE WORLD—PART ONE

2 THESSALONIANS 2:3-14

³ LET NO ONE DECEIVE YOU BY ANY MEANS; FOR THAT DAY WILL NOT COME UNLESS THE FALLING AWAY COMES FIRST, AND THE MAN OF SIN IS REVEALED, THE SON OF PERDITION, ⁴ WHO OPPOSES AND EXALTS HIMSELF ABOVE ALL THAT IS CALLED GOD OR THAT IS WORSHIPED, SO THAT HE SITS AS GOD IN THE TEMPLE OF GOD, SHOWING HIMSELF THAT HE IS GOD. ⁵ DO YOU NOT REMEMBER THAT WHEN I WAS STILL WITH YOU I TOLD YOU THESE THINGS? ⁶ AND NOW YOU KNOW WHAT IS RESTRAINING, THAT HE MAY BE REVEALED IN HIS OWN TIME. ⁷ FOR THE MYSTERY OF LAWLESSNESS IS ALREADY AT WORK; ONLY HE WHO NOW RESTRAINS WILL DO SO UNTIL HE IS TAKEN OUT OF THE WAY. ⁸ AND THEN THE LAWLESS ONE WILL BE REVEALED, WHOM THE LORD WILL CONSUME WITH THE BREATH OF HIS MOUTH AND DESTROY WITH THE BRIGHTNESS OF HIS COMING. ⁹ THE COMING OF THE LAWLESS ONE IS ACCORDING TO THE WORKING OF SATAN, WITH ALL POWER, SIGNS, AND LYING WONDERS, ¹⁰ AND WITH ALL UNRIGHTEOUS DECEPTION AMONG THOSE WHO PERISH, BECAUSE THEY DID NOT RECEIVE THE LOVE OF THE TRUTH, THAT THEY MIGHT BE SAVED. ¹¹ AND FOR THIS REASON GOD WILL SEND THEM STRONG DELUSION, THAT THEY SHOULD BELIEVE THE LIE, ¹² THAT THEY ALL MAY BE CONDEMNED WHO DID NOT BELIEVE THE TRUTH BUT HAD PLEASURE IN UNRIGHTEOUSNESS. ¹³ BUT WE ARE BOUND TO GIVE THANKS TO GOD ALWAYS FOR YOU, BRETHREN BELOVED BY THE LORD, BECAUSE GOD FROM THE BEGINNING CHOSE YOU FOR SALVATION THROUGH SANCTIFICATION BY THE SPIRIT AND BELIEF IN THE TRUTH, ¹⁴ TO WHICH HE CALLED YOU BY OUR GOSPEL, FOR THE OBTAINING OF THE GLORY OF OUR LORD JESUS CHRIST.

1. Two events will take place before the return of the Lord. First, there will be a _____ _____ or an apostasy of the church. Second, the son of _____ will be revealed.

2. The abomination of desolation is when _____ walks into the newly built temple in Jerusalem and proclaims he is the _____. This proclamation from Antichrist begins what we know as _____ _____.

3. Antichrist comes with the workings of _____, in all power and signs and lying wonders. His deception will lead to _____ and _____ toward God and His Word.

4. During this time, _____ sends delusion onto humanity so they would believe Satan's lie. God is _____ those who love Him and pursue _____ from those who believe the lie. God creates a very clear line in this separation with no gray area.

5. The _____ is presented through leaders and teachers of the _____, but the world presents lies to us, and we have to make a choice. We make the choice by setting _____ and standards in our lives based on studying the Bible.

6. God is going to reject the _____ church. We cannot stand in the middle and never fully commit to living lives with great _____ for Christ. Each of us has a _____ to perform in the body of Christ and we must be all-in for Jesus because He was all-in for us.

7. Jesus interacted with those who should have recognized Him as the _____ and told them there are two fathers. His Father is in heaven but their father is _____. They each have a voice, and they were listening to the _____ of the devil.

8. The Apostle Peter was _____ by two fathers, his old father before _____ and his current Father, God. We need to understand that we can be influenced just as well. We must be able to _____ what is of God and what is not of God.

9. Satan's voice will seem very familiar to us because it will identify with our fleshly _____. At times, God's voice will not make _____ to us, but we go with it in faith. We look _____ to the world because they listen and obey Satan's voice.

10. The doctrine Satan presented to Eve put her in a situation of _____ _____. It brought her to a place where she began to question God and His Word. She had no fear of _____ for her sin and she followed her _____ by going after material things.

11. The church today teaches believers that we are supposed to live lives of extreme _____, but this is not what Jesus told us. Our prayers to bring something from heaven to earth should be for the _____ of expanding the Kingdom of God and not for our comfort or pleasure.

12. A _____ is a fleeting moment—it's something that comes and goes. _____ are thoughts that remain in our mind as we meditate on them. A _____ is something that becomes part of us. _____ starts as a thought that we begin to imagine, and when acted upon, becomes a stronghold.

13. The _____ for Christians is the Word of God, which helps us bring every thought into _____. But we have to know and recognize the Word in order for it to be an effective filter in our lives. The Word is _____, and truth will set us free from the _____ of this world.

KEY WORDS:

(a) Lukewarm   (b) Separation   (c) Reprobate Mind   (d) Doctrine   (e) Imaginations

_____ One that is rejected by God for suppressing the truth by their wickedness.

_____ Creations of the mind triggered by a mental thought.

_____ Coolness toward faith and belief in God, not zealous, indifferent.

_____ Set of beliefs in religious denominations taught or believed to be true.

_____ Division of those who belong to God and those who belong to the world.

SESSION ANSWERS:

1. falling away, perdition
2. Antichrist, Messiah, great tribulation
3. Satan, unrighteousness, disobedience
4. God, separating, truth
5. truth, world, boundaries
6. lukewarm, passion, function
7. Messiah, Satan, voice
8. influenced, salvation, discern
9. urges, sense, foolish
10. false security, consequences, flesh
11. comfort, purpose
12. thought, Imaginations, stronghold
13. filter, obedience, truth, strongholds

KEY WORD ANSWERS:

c, e, a, d, b

PERSONAL DEVOTION – DAY 1

EXPOSE THE TRUTH

READ: 2 THESSALONIANS 2

Look at Verse 1, because it sets the tone for the whole chapter. It speaks of the return of our Lord and the gathering of Believers unto Him. Paul is writing this letter because the Thessalonians were upset. They thought the Lord was returning in their time. In fact, there were fraudulent letters being circulated from the false apostles, telling them that the Lord was returning or that the Lord had returned. Here, Paul exposes the truth and through the Holy Spirit, lays out a timeline and a sequence of how end time events will occur.

In Verse 3, Paul says the Lord's return will not come unless there comes a great apostasy first. Apostasy means deserting the faith. This is the same sequence we see in, Matthew 24, where Jesus lays out end time events.

Jesus chronologically prophesied the same timeline; apostasy in the Church, many are offended, false doctrine, false prophets, false teachers, and the Bible says that the love of many will wax cold. Then in, Verse 15 of Matthew 24, Antichrist is revealed and great tribulation begins.

This timeline is foundational when studying end times.

Paul is very specific in, 2 Thessalonians 2:4-8, that there is a great falling away first. Unfortunately, this may be the most misunderstood Scripture in Western end times teaching.

The false assumption is that Paul is speaking about the rapture. That is clearly not the case, because of the word he uses is: *apostacia*.

Paul describes the Church diminishing to a point where Antichrist is released. People have a hard time getting their arms wrapped around this, but he is not changing the subject matter because he reiterates again. The Church has to be weakened. That is the apostasy.

This is why Jesus continues to repeat, "do not be deceived," in His warning to the Church. He describes the deception as so great, and the turmoil so great, that even the very elect will be moved by it.

We have to be able to discern right from wrong and be steadfast in our faith.

PERSONAL DEVOTION – DAY 2

STRONG DELUSION

READ: 2 THESSALONIANS 2:9-13

In these four verses, we see that Antichrist comes employed by Satan, with all power and great wonders. His deception will be hallmarked by the miraculous, and his great ability to persuade people to believe him to be God.

In Verse 11, we read, "And for this cause God shall send them strong delusion, that they should believe a lie."

God sends a delusion? What does this mean? Does God actually help Satan deceive the world?

God uses the deception to separate those who have a love for truth from those that believe a lie. He's creating a clear boundary. Many will be offended throughout this time.

This is almost counterintuitive to the way we think of God, because God is actually sending delusion to the earth that will be accepted by those who do not love the truth or know the truth causing this separation.

This delusion will enhance the apostasy. God is going to make it crystal clear who belongs to Him and who does not.

If you back up from this and look at the delusion as a giant filter, than we can see that God will use the "delusion filter" to purify His Church. This will make Believers pure in their faith and in their devotion to Him.

God is basically saying, "I am going to separate you until there is no gray area, you are either with Me and you love My Word, or you are not." There is no middle ground with God.

God wants a bride who is fully committed to Him. God wants Christians who are on fire for Him and passionate about His Word. Not lukewarm pew-filling church-goers.

How can you make sure you are devoted to the Lord?

How can you protect yourself from the great delusion?

Does this inspire you to fear the Lord? Why?

PERSONAL DEVOTION – DAY 3

BORN IN DARKNESS

READ: JOHN 8

Have you ever found yourself stumbling around the house in the middle of the night? It's amazing how a night light is so helpful when you wake up in the dark.

Jesus comes to us, trapped in a world of darkness and tells us if we will look to Him, He will be the light we need. We don't have to stumble along. In fact, His light not only will illuminate our path now, but His light will lead us to everlasting life.

Paul says that we were born in darkness. We were blind. We did not see the truth and glory of God, and we did not have the ability or the desire to see our sin nature.

We didn't sense our need for a Savior, so we lived selfishly for our own pleasure, avoiding the thought of death and eternity.

When God saved us, He opened our eyes to see, "…the light of the knowledge of the glory of God in the face of Christ" (2 Corinthians 4:6).

Paul wisely taught, "Be not overcome of evil, but overcome evil with good" (Romans 12:21).

"…while we wait for the blessed hope – the appearing of the glory of our great God and Savior, Jesus Christ, who gave himself for us to redeem us from all wickedness and to purify for himself a people that are his very own, eager to do what is good" (Titus 2:13-14).

"Let perseverance finish its work so that you may be mature and complete, not lacking anything" (James 1:4).

"Do not be afraid of what you are about to suffer. I tell you, the devil will put some of you in prison to test you, and you will suffer persecution for ten days. Be faithful, even to the point of death, and I will give you life as your victor's crown" (Revelation 2:10).

As the world gets darker, we must allow His light to shine on us and through us.

PERSONAL DEVOTION – DAY 4

GUARD YOUR THOUGHTS

READ: 2 CORINTHIANS 10:3-5

In this chapter, we are told that there is an internal war against our flesh. As humans, we are subject to thoughts, imaginations and strongholds.

A thought is a fleeting moment; it comes and goes. An imagination is a thought that remains; it rolls around in your mind and causes you to meditate on it. Finally, a stronghold is something that has been actively meditated upon; it can oftentimes become a part of the fabric of your being.

Let's look at sin, because sin starts as a thought, you begin to imagine the thought and when you act upon the thought enough times it becomes a part of who you are.

Just for example, let's examine the sin of adultery. You do not wake up one Wednesday morning and think; Well, today is Wednesday so I am going to commit adultery!

That's just silly.

Sin starts with a thought and you begin to imagine it by thinking about committing adultery.

Remember, Jesus taught us, that if you look after a woman in lust then you have already committed adultery because it is now a part of your thought process.

Next, you act upon your imagination, and yes, the first time it is difficult but ten times later it has become a part of who you are.

Jesus gives us instructions to take into captivity every thought to the obedience of God's Word.

The filter for our thoughts must be the Word of God.

This is why it is important to study the Word. Jesus told us to meditate on the Word and to continue in the Word, "Then you will know the truth and the truth will set you free" (John 8:32).

It's also important to make sure your filter is good! For instance, if your filter is based on wrong doctrine, then your ability to filter what is right and what is wrong gets thrown off balance.

PERSONAL DEVOTION – DAY 5

NARROW IS THE PATH

READ: MATTHEW 17

You do not have to be a rocket scientist to understand the mathematical difference between the words *many* and *few*. Jesus also tells us that broad is the way to destruction and narrow is the path to salvation. This doesn't sound like a tough lesson to learn. He makes it pretty clear that it's easy to choose the wrong path and many will do so.

Our way is Jesus Christ and our path is a narrow and specific path according to God's Word. Jesus said, "…I am the way, the truth, and the life…" (John 14:6). There is no other way to God but through Jesus Christ and it is on God's terms.

Jesus tells us that there are many wrong paths and that Satan is the father of them all. Such as; the Muslims, the Buddhists, the Atheists and all other religions. Each of these doctrines offers a different path. However, there is only one way to Him.

Are you sure you're on the right path? Does saying a prayer in a Target® parking lot, asking Jesus into your life, put you on the right path? Forever?

Think about Judas. He attended every service, volunteered, and served as the Temple treasurer. However, would you consider naming your child Judas? Would you say Judas was on the right path?

It's not likely. Judas is often a man associated with evil. Judas was not on God's path. He was going through the motions. God requires more than lip-service. He requires Lordship; this means that you must follow His Word, His purpose and His plan – not yours.

You can go through the motions and label yourself a Christian throughout your entire life and absolutely have no salvation in you at all!

This is a very, very, scary thought isn't it? But it is not scary if you read the Bible and understand that we have an obligation to know God's Word and to have a relationship with the Lord.

Our relationship with God is like a marriage. It is not like joining a club or some group that you visit by raising your hand and saying a prayer.

Your relationship with the Lord is a total commitment to Him. It is being all-in and giving to Him your life because you believe that He is your Lord and Savior!

SESSION 6

A CHURCH THAT LOOKS LIKE THE WORLD –PART TWO

SESSION 6
A CHURCH THAT LOOKS LIKE THE WORLD—PART TWO

2 PETER 2:14-22

¹⁴ HAVING EYES FULL OF ADULTERY AND THAT CANNOT CEASE FROM SIN, ENTICING UNSTABLE SOULS. THEY HAVE A HEART TRAINED IN COVETOUS PRACTICES, AND ARE ACCURSED CHILDREN. ¹⁵ THEY HAVE FORSAKEN THE RIGHT WAY AND GONE ASTRAY, FOLLOWING THE WAY OF BALAAM THE SON OF BEOR, WHO LOVED THE WAGES OF UNRIGHTEOUSNESS; ¹⁶ BUT HE WAS REBUKED FOR HIS INIQUITY: A DUMB DONKEY SPEAKING WITH A MAN'S VOICE RESTRAINED THE MADNESS OF THE PROPHET. ¹⁷ THESE ARE WELLS WITHOUT WATER, CLOUDS CARRIED BY A TEMPEST, FOR WHOM IS RESERVED THE BLACKNESS OF DARKNESS FOREVER. ¹⁸ FOR WHEN THEY SPEAK GREAT SWELLING WORDS OF EMPTINESS, THEY ALLURE THROUGH THE LUSTS OF THE FLESH, THROUGH LEWDNESS, THE ONES WHO HAVE ACTUALLY ESCAPED FROM THOSE WHO LIVE IN ERROR. ¹⁹ WHILE THEY PROMISE THEM LIBERTY, THEY THEMSELVES ARE SLAVES OF CORRUPTION; FOR BY WHOM A PERSON IS OVERCOME, BY HIM ALSO HE IS BROUGHT INTO BONDAGE. ²⁰ FOR IF, AFTER THEY HAVE ESCAPED THE POLLUTIONS OF THE WORLD THROUGH THE KNOWLEDGE OF THE LORD AND SAVIOR JESUS CHRIST, THEY ARE AGAIN ENTANGLED IN THEM AND OVERCOME, THE LATTER END IS WORSE FOR THEM THAN THE BEGINNING. ²¹ FOR IT WOULD HAVE BEEN BETTER FOR THEM NOT TO HAVE KNOWN THE WAY OF RIGHTEOUSNESS, THAN HAVING KNOWN IT, TO TURN FROM THE HOLY COMMANDMENT DELIVERED TO THEM. ²² BUT IT HAS HAPPENED TO THEM ACCORDING TO THE TRUE PROVERB: "A DOG RETURNS TO HIS OWN VOMIT," AND, "A SOW, HAVING WASHED, TO HER WALLOWING IN THE MIRE."

---

1. There is a _____ perception in Christianity about what truth is and the _____ use of the word "love." We have misused the word today to such an extent that everyone has their own _____ of what love means.

2. We may define love one way and someone else may describe it another way, but the only way we can define the love of God is to know the _____. We must look at what God's Word tells us and not make _____ based on history or _____.

3. When we read "God so loved the world," it means God loves _____ and He loves His _____. God loves the world, but we can't assume God loves every single person in the world. God loves those who _____ in His Son Jesus Christ, and that does not include _____.

4. If we don't understand the love of God we can easily be _____. We have to grasp what His Word says about love because one day the _____ of God is going to be equally important to us as the love of God. There is the _____ of God and there is the _____ of God.

5. The early church dealt with the saved and the unsaved in a very direct way. They were told to listen and _____ in the Gospel message, _____ and be baptized, and believe in Jesus Christ. Not once is the word _____ mentioned in the book of Acts.

6. The promises in the _____ are addressed to those who believe in Jesus Christ. _____ cannot take hold of the promises of God because the letters were not addressed to them. But they can repent and believe in Jesus; then His promises are _____ _____ to them.

7. God is no _____ of persons, but keep in mind God has an _____, and His opinion toward everyone is not the same. God shows no _____, but everyone who fears and respects Him and lives according to His Word is accepted by Him.

8. Our culture has modified God's Word and His character to the extent that many have a false perception of _____, and society has become _____ of things that God _____. Trust me, God does not change for us, we must change for God.

9. Born-again Christians who have escaped the _____ of the world through the knowledge of Jesus Christ but become _____ again with the world will receive a higher level of judgment. They would've been better off to have never known rather than to turn away from the _____.

10. We are saved by faith, and the love and mercy of God brings us into _____. But to say there is no _____ upon us after commitment to Jesus is a false assumption. We are to experience _____ growth in our relationship with God and live as Christ lived.

11. We are to seek first the _____ __ _____ and His righteousness. It is a lack of faith when we chase after worldly things for our own _____. Our prayers for material wealth are seen by God as _____ prayers. Our prayers should be for valid and righteous needs only.

12. We are all guilty of adulterous prayers, but through revelation knowledge we find true _____ in God's plan for our lives. When we are content and have no _____ is when we live without _____ and live in _____ knowing God will provide for all our needs.

KEY WORDS:

(a) Contentment (b) Gospel (c) Entangled (d) Tolerant (e) Epistle

_____ Involved in unrighteousness that is difficult to escape from.

_____ Willing to accept other beliefs without criticism even if you disagree.

_____ Satisfied with what you have and who you are in Christ Jesus.

_____ Message of salvation that Christ died for us; known as the good news.

_____ Formal letter written to the early Church by one of the Apostles.

SESSION ANSWERS:

1. false, incorrect, definition
2. truth, assumptions, emotions
3. humanity, creation, believe, everyone
4. deceived, judgment, goodness, severity
5. believe, repent, love
6. Epistles, unbelievers, freely given
7. respecter, opinion, partiality
8. God, tolerant, loathes
9. corruption, entangled, truth
10. salvation, expectation, continuous
11. Kingdom of God, consumption, adulterous
12. contentment, lack, fear, peace

KEY WORD ANSWERS:

c, d, a, b, e

PERSONAL DEVOTION – DAY 1

THE TRUTH ABOUT LOVE

READ: JOHN 3:15-21;36 // ACTS 10:34-35

There are some doctrines within the Church that send a false perception of truth. One example of this is the modern-day perception of "love". We have misused this word to such an extent that it's difficult to give a clear definition.

What is your definition of love?

The Bible says that God loved the world, meaning that He loved humanity and creation. Yet, every human being is condemned to death and the wrath of God is already upon them. Verse 36, expounds on this. What we see is that God loved the world, but we assume that He loves each person. Remember, God is ultimately a Judge.

The Book of Acts is filled with the acts of men and women who have the Spirit of God in and upon them. On the day of Pentecost, the Spirit of God came upon the apostles, the disciples, and the one hundred and twenty men and women in the upper room, and then, from that point forward all the others who joined the Church.

As the numbers of the Church grew, we see how they learned to operate and function, how they dealt with the saved and unsaved, and how they dealt with issues amongst each other. We see the healings and other things that Jesus did, and then, we see them done in the Book of Acts by Believers, men and women who are empowered by the Holy Spirit.

When new Believers asked Peter about what should they do once they heard the Gospel, Peter told them to repent and be baptized and believe in Jesus Christ!

Repent.

Not once is the word *love* mentioned in the Book of Acts when the disciples are compelling people to follow Christ.

So, every time they were confronted with salvation or with someone asking what they should do to be saved their answer was to turn back to God, turn your life around, and repent. Turning around is the action of faith in repentance or true salvation.

You see, when you have a false perception of love you do not repent or take action when you must do something, understand that this false perception sets the stage where there is no expectation on you. Yet, here in the Bible it tells us that there is an expectation on us and that we must turn around and head toward Christ and become obedient toward His Word.

PERSONAL DEVOTION – DAY 2
HEED THE WORD

READ: 1 CHRONICLES 13

In the first few verses, we read that the people of God sought to bring the Ark of God back to Jerusalem. The people were very excited about this and had it been a democracy; it would have been in favor by at least a two-thirds vote.

As the Ark entered the city, the people put on their party clothes and began singing, dancing and praising God. It was a worship service, and rightly so. But in the middle of this celebratory procession, God struck somebody dead.

Flat out, dead. This seems a bit shocking.

Why do you think God did this?

A few chapters later, we read that God had given specific instructions to the Levites in regards to the Ark. The people had disobeyed God's Word in the way it was carried and the way that it was transported to the city. It's important to understand that God doesn't care what our intentions were. He is not going to change His Word for us.

God didn't change His Word even though His covenant people had sincere intentions.

We must know the Word of God and not make assumptions that our attitude or emotions will save us. Only God's Word will save us. When we misuse words, such as, love or grace in situations where repentance and change are required, it's a big mistake. We need to use severity. And, when we do not use severity than we change God's Word and when we do not teach the Word of God the way it is written and the way it is supposed to be understood then those listening will have a false perception of things in their lives.

Our culture has come to a place where we have modified God's Word so much, and Who God is, that there is a great deal of false perception of Him today. People have become tolerant of things that God hates.

Newsflash: God does not change for man so we have to find out what His Word says and go with His Word.

Today make an effort to understand God's Word because your life could depend on it!

PERSONAL DEVOTION – DAY 3

NO GRAY AREA

READ: 2 PETER 2

Peter discusses false leaders in this chapter. He points out that these leaders are adulterous, meaning, they are disregarding the covenant. We clearly read in, Verses 20 through 22, that there is no gray area with God. There is God's way and everything else.

What do you see as the most dangerous doctrinal teaching of the modern-day Church?

I believe that the "once saved, always saved" doctrine is lethal to the modern Church. Hebrews 6:4 -8, Ephesians 2:4-5, Ephesians 8-9 and Ephesians 5:1-8, all offer validation that salvation can be lost.

These verses of Scripture are very clear with no gray area. Believers in Christ have escaped the corruption in the world through the knowledge of the Gospel and if they become entangled again they will fall into a worse judgment.

That's harsh! But it's the standard that God has set for those who know the truth and turn away from it.

Nowhere in the Bible does it say, "once saved, always saved." In fact, it says it would have been better for them not to have known the way then to have known it and to have turned from it.

These are New Testament writings. Even the most vocal of the disciples, Peter, wrote in his closing letter to the Church that there would be teachers teaching covetous practices and they are teaching things that are of adultery. The things they teach are not right because they are things that touch on what the flesh urges rather than on what the Word of God tells us.

How does someone have a sense of security that they are really saved? Salvation is not an event; it is a lifelong process. Similar to marriage. You can't just get married and only be married on Sundays. You have to work and improve your marriage every day. Continue to put time and effort into the relationship. It's about sacrifice and submission. Saying, you are my Lord and Savior and I submit to You and Your will. It is by grace and faith and His mercy and love that gave us the ability to come into salvation.

It is critical to understand that by faith, and through grace, we can be saved. We have to uphold our covenant with Christ and grow in our walk with Him.

PERSONAL DEVOTION – DAY 4

ADULTEROUS PRAYERS

READ: 1 JOHN 2:15-22 // JAMES 4:3-8

John talks about the lust of the flesh. Remember Eve? She thought the fruit was good for food and she saw that it was pleasant to the eye and she felt it would make her wise. These are the three different things that went through her mind.

John is saying, love not the world or the things in the world and do not lust for those things or chase or pursue those things because if you do than the love of the Father is not in you.

Then John goes immediately from telling us not to love the world or the things of the world, into Antichrist. And what does John say about the spirit of Antichrist? What John is saying here is that you should not love or pursue the things in the world, and do not let the pride of life or the lust of your flesh drive your ambitions, and do not allow compromise in your life because this is all the spirit of Antichrist. This spirit is leading you away from the things of God.

In James 4, we learn that asking is praying.

James is saying that you ask and you receive not that you would consume it upon your own lust. Let's stop and think this through because the Bible says that you are asking for something in prayer, yet, you are not receiving it.

Why is it that you are not receiving it? Well, you are not receiving it because you are asking for the wrong thing. Maybe you missed the target.

Well, let me tell you, there are people who have written books about this! So, what is James talking about when he calls those who pray such prayers; *adulterers* and *adulteresses*?

James is saying that you are in a covenant with God and you have made an agreement with God so that you have become one with Him. Therefore, God is saying, "I live in you and you live in Me and when you pray for things that are worldly or look to the world to provide you pleasure then you are an enemy to Me." So, when this happens what are you doing? You are committing spiritual adultery and you are praying for material things in your life in order to consume them upon your own lusts.

Jesus tells us in, Matthew 6:33, "But seek ye first the Kingdom of God, and his righteousness; and all these things shall be added unto you." Jesus tells us that it is a lack of faith to chase worldly things. Listen to me carefully because good people have written books about the prosperity Gospel, yet, the Word of God tells us that the greatest man born of woman until the time of Jesus was a homeless man, John the Baptist!

PERSONAL DEVOTION – DAY 5

LIVE FOR GOD

READ: JAMES 1:2-4

What does perfect and entire, wanting nothing, mean? It means that you see no lack in your life which is good, because when you see yourself lacking something, then you see yourself in fear.

Now, this happens to all of us but the Bible tells us that by faith and patience we will have true contentment with God, and contentment is peace. Being content with what you have puts you in a place where you do not fear and you trust in God to provide.

God loves each and every one of us. Though, to have a genuine relationship with Him, it must be on His terms.

Yes, salvation is great and it is the greatest gift from God, and yes, it is by faith, and yes, He forgives you of your sins, but there is an expectation on you to decide to make Jesus Christ your Lord and Savior, now and forever.

This expectation on you requires you to live the life of holiness seeking Him with a spirit of humility and submission!

Are you living a life for Him?

Daniel 11:31-35, outlines that to know Him throughout great tribulation is a testament to your commitment. It is important that you form a relationship with Him so that in this chaotic time, you can aid others in their relationship with Christ.

Today, take time to pray:

"Father, we thank You for this time of fellowship. We thank You for this Word, Lord God, and we thank You, Father, that You have given us a revelation of what truth is. We thank You, Father, that You continue to lead us and guide us in all truth. To reveal Your Word to us and to give us understanding and wisdom. Father, we pray that You continue to bless our efforts to bring truth and life and light that is rightly divided and anointed of You. We thank You in Jesus' Name. Amen."

SESSION 7
GREAT TRIBULATION

SESSION 7

GREAT TRIBULATION

MATTHEW 24:15-26

¹⁵ "Therefore when you see the 'abomination of desolation,' spoken of by Daniel the prophet, standing in the holy place" (whoever reads, let him understand), ¹⁶ then let those who are in Judea flee to the mountains. ¹⁷ Let him who is on the housetop not go down to take anything out of his house. ¹⁸ And let him who is in the field not go back to get his clothes. ¹⁹ But woe to those who are pregnant and to those who are nursing babies in those days! ²⁰ And pray that your flight may not be in winter or on the Sabbath. ²¹ For then there will be great tribulation, such as has not been since the beginning of the world until this time, no, nor ever shall be. ²² And unless those days were shortened, no flesh would be saved; but for the elect's sake those days will be shortened. ²³ Then if anyone says to you, 'Look, here is the Christ!' or 'There!' do not believe it.

²⁴ For false christs and false prophets will rise and show great signs and wonders to deceive, if possible, even the elect. ²⁵ See, I have told you beforehand. ²⁶ Therefore if they say to you, 'Look, He is in the desert!' do not go out; or 'Look, He is in the inner rooms!' do not believe it.

---

1. Great tribulation begins with Antichrist going into the temple and proclaiming to be the Messiah. His _____ is set up in the temple where the place of God would be. His action _____ the temple and it is called the _____ _____ _____.

2. Immediately following the desecration, chaos spreads very quickly in the area of _____ or _____. Jesus warns those who live in that region of the world to flee into the _____. Don't even go home to pack any belongings because there will be no _____.

3. Satan gives Antichrist his _____, his _____, and his _____ _____ for the last three-and-a-half years of great tribulation. The authority that Satan has, which is given to him by _____, will be transferred over to this man, Antichrist, who will rule here on earth.

4. Jesus and Antichrist have an equal amount of time empowered by their _____ here on earth. Jesus came to the earth in love to bring peace and _____. Antichrist first brings _____ peace but then he brings global _____ and world domination.

5. The false prophet points to the image of Antichrist and orders everyone to pay _____ or salute the image in worship. Antichrist will control religion in his _____ and if you live in his territory you must lay aside any _____ that does not allow you to put him first.

6. One at a time, the seven seals on the scroll will be broken by _____. The earth is overtaken by war and _____, famine and _____, and the _____ of the field come into the cities looking for food. We are now in great tribulation and the counterfeit peace has been left behind.

7. After the seven seals, God brings forth His _____ on the earth in the seven trumpets. At the same time, Antichrist is on earth _____ the Christians and the Jews. God's purpose is set _____ for Antichrist just as it was in the days of Moses and Pharaoh.

8. When the fifth angel sounds its trumpet, we are told there will be special _____ for Believers from the wrath of God. Remember, there was _____ for God's people while He was transacting the plagues upon the _____ and we will have that same peace during tribulation.

9. We must not look at this as a time to _____ because it will be a great _____ to work with God being in the center of His will. We are to _____ and do the work we are called to do for His glory that is the Great Commission.

10. We are to preach the Gospel and bring about inner peace while trying to _____ the hearts and minds of those who do not know the _____ because they will be overwhelmed by these events. We will not be overwhelmed because we have _____ _____.

11. After the wrath of God begins, we are told that prayers from the _____ on earth are being sent up to heaven. This means _____ are here during great tribulation, so we must prepare ourselves in _____ for these events to help others who are not equipped and ready.

12. An army of _____ soldiers will oppose Antichrist during great tribulation. A 200-million man army will move toward the _____ _____ _____ and the battle takes place in _____. In the midst of all the turmoil there will be nations who will oppose Antichrist.

13. At the end, there are two Saints believed to be _____ and _____, who are killed and the whole world views their dead bodies on the streets. The earth is covered in absolute carnage and the _____ dead on earth throw a party and exchange gifts in celebration.

14. Imagine how _____ and spiritually dead the earth will be at that time. It is difficult to image that after the seven _____, seven _____, seven _____, the destruction of Antichrist, and the wrath of God that there will still be those who will not _____ God was behind all the events!

KEY WORDS:

(a) Plague   (b) Great Commission   (c) Armageddon   (d) Pestilence   (e) Valley of Megiddo

_____ Instructions of the resurrected Christ to His disciples to spread the Gospel to all nations.

_____ Site of the final battle between Jesus Christ and Satan.

_____ Disease or affliction sent as a divine chastisement or the judgment of God.

_____ Where the last battle between good and evil is fought before Judgment Day.

_____ Disease causing widespread crop damage or animal deaths.

SESSION ANSWERS:

1. image, desecrates, abomination of desolation
2. Judea, Jerusalem, mountains, time
3. power, seat, great authority, God
4. fathers, salvation, counterfeit, warfare
5. homage, domain, belief
6. Jesus, turmoil, pestilence, beasts
7. wrath, eradicating, opposition
8. protection, peace, Egyptians
9. fear, opportunity, persevere
10. stabilize, truth, revelation knowledge
11. saints, believers, advance
12. unsaved, Valley of Megiddo, Armageddon
13. Moses, Elijah, spiritually
14. corrupt, seals, trumpets, vials, recognize

KEY WORD ANSWERS:

b, e, a, c, d

PERSONAL DEVOTION – DAY 1

THE SPIRIT OF ANTICHRIST

READ: REVELATION 13

Just before the return of Christ, we learn that there is a seven-year period of tribulation. The latter half is called: Great Tribulation. This period begins with Antichrist entering the Temple and the abomination of desolation. An image is erected of Antichrist in the Temple and this will replace the image of God.

John describes the events in, Revelation 13:1-2, as that of a beast rising out of the sea. The beast has seven heads that respectively represent the seven world dominating kingdoms that have an Antichrist spirit of leadership. These kingdoms persecuted the Chosen People – the Jews. Further, John describes the ten horns on the beast. Each of the horns represent a nation controlled by Antichrist.

Now, if you go back in history you can count the Egyptians, the Assyrians, the Babylonians, the Medo-Persians, the Greeks, and the Romans, as dominating kingdoms whose spirit of leadership was that of Antichrist. Those six nations were ruled by a single man who was thought to be a god and a man. For instance, Rome was ruled by Caesar who was a dictator and he was thought to be part deity and part humanity. Then in Egypt there was Pharaoh, and in Babylon there was Nebuchadnezzar, and these men were also thought to be part deity and part humanity. All of them persecuted, attacked and abused God's covenant people. Out of the seven heads, six were just mentioned; this leaves one yet to come which is Antichrist.

The Bible tells us that this image of Antichrist has ten horns on his head, this represents the control of ten separate nations and his nation is to be the eleventh nation. These ten nations are going to give their power and sovereignty to Antichrist and he will control them. He is also going to actually consume three of these nations and this is what the ten horns on the beast represent.

Scripture then takes us from looking at the beast to looking at a man because even though these nations were separate, each one of them will be controlled by a single man. Look at Pharaoh and how he had supreme authority over Egypt and how he could do whatever he wanted because he was the law in that nation.

This whole chapter is about Antichrist coming on the scene and the False Prophet. We also see something else that happens. We see that Satan gives Antichrist his power, his seat and his great authority for his three and a half year time period, which is the last half of great tribulation. All of the authority that Satan has which is given to him by God will be transferred over to this man, Antichrist, who will rule here on earth.

The entirety of, Revelation 13, describes Antichrist's rise to power. It's important to understand that Satan will give Antichrist his power, seat and authority.

PERSONAL DEVOTION – DAY 2

THE GIVER OF ALL THINGS

READ: REVELATION 13

We read many times in, Revelation 13, that power is given to the beast. You need to understand Who gives things unto him.

It is God.

God allows Satan his time here on the earth. And, the reason why God allows Antichrist three and a half years is because Jesus had three plus years for His ministry. Therefore, each of the seeds, the Son of God and the son of Satan, has an equal amount of time empowered by their fathers here on the earth to do their father's will.

Of course, Jesus came in love to bring peace and salvation, but Antichrist first brings a counterfeit peace, and then, he brings war because he wants world domination.

This power that the dragon, who is Satan, gives Antichrist along with his seat and his authority will be released for the forty-two months and it is an extraordinary amount of power that he will have while walking here on the earth.

He was also given the power to make war with Saints, who are Believers, and to overcome them.

Where else in Scripture do we see that Satan was given the power to overcome a Believer? We see that it happened in the Book of Job. Antichrist will have power to make war with us and to overcome us and this point needs to be very clear to you so that you can understand it is God Who is allowing this to happen.

It is important to notice that a second beast comes from the earth and this is the False Prophet who is a different entity than Antichrist. The False Prophet persuades and initiates global devotion of Antichrist.

This section of Scripture can get a little messy so here is a recent example in history that is better understood:

Picture Adolf Hitler walking into a room. The reaction of the German public would be; *Heil Hitler*. When Antichrist rises to power, the False Prophet will point to him and initiate a salute, or a measure of worship. Then, all of society under the control of Antichrist will be required to obey this command. What does this absolute control imply?

Antichrist will control all religion and politics within the region that he dominates. Antichrist will also control the commerce within his region. Those without a specific marking will not be permitted to buy or sell in the marketplace.

We must not be intimidated by this news, but rather understand that offering our lives to God is the ultimate act of praise and worship.

PERSONAL DEVOTION – DAY 3

THE SEALS ARE BROKEN

READ: REVELATION 6

Picture a scroll with seven seals on it and we do not know what is in the scroll, but when Jesus begins to open the scroll, one seal at a time, John sees that something happens in the earth every time a seal is broken. Antichrist is released when the first seal is broken and he is wearing a crown, meaning, he is a political leader. He also carries a bow but he has no arrows, meaning, he is not going out to make war because his strategy is to conquer through peace and flattery. Remember, Antichrist does not come initially on the scene to cause conflict or war because he brings about peace.

The next seal is opened and we see a world war. Then, we see rampant inflation and food shortages and a whole day's wages will only feed one person. Next, we see more war and more famine and more pestilence. We see beasts of the field coming into the cities because they are starving from a lack of food. We are now in great tribulation because we have left peace behind.

The fifth seal are, Verses 9 and 10, and it speaks of those who are waiting under the altar. They are the Believers who were slain for the Word of God during the tribulation period. We see that there are Saints in heaven underneath the altar of God saying, "Hey, how much longer is this going to go on?" They are wondering when will God avenge us and they are told to wait until your brethren who are still on earth should also be fulfilled. This means in, Verse 11, that there are still Believers in the earth. The slain Believers are told to wait.

God then opens another seal and there is a great earthquake and the sun turns black. This brings us to the great wrath of God which are the seven trumpets. At the same time, Antichrist is on the earth following his agenda to eradicate Christians and Jews.

Meanwhile, God is sending disaster on the earth to kill a third part of the grass. Then, God sends another disaster to kill a third part of the water along with the fish that live in the sea. We learn that God is transacting these events on the earth, but why? The reason why God is doing this is because He is setting opposition for Antichrist just as it was in the days of Moses. In fact, there is some protection here for Believers just as it was in the days of Moses.

This content can seem paralyzing. However, it's important to remember that God has given us His playbook. As Believers, we can identify what is happening and what we need to prepare for.

It is important to view this as an opportunity to serve God and fully act out the Great Commission. We are instructed to share His Word, always aiming to stabilize the hearts and minds of those who do not know the truth.

PERSONAL DEVOTION – DAY 4

THE TWO SAINTS

READ: REVELATION 11

I want to show you something that I find incredibly amazing. We believe the two witnesses are Moses and Elijah.

Verse 5, sounds like Elijah because he called down fire from heaven.

Verse 6, sounds like Moses because he changed water to blood and he brought different plagues on the earth.

The forty-two months is extremely consistent in Scripture with no deviation and it is also the longest amount of time. I believe this time will be shortened somewhat because we read in, Matthew 24:22, that unless those days be shorten there shall be no flesh saved.

The second thing I want to point out is at the end of tribulation these two Saints, whether they are Moses and Elijah or whoever they might be, are killed and the whole world views them.

At this point, we are at the end of tribulation so all of the destruction has happened, and the earth is covered in complete carnage. These two Saints are dead and they that dwell upon the earth send gifts to one another, they have a party over their death!

Think about this for a moment, and consider how at the end of tribulation, these folks still cannot see the truth! They cannot identify God.

Imagine how corrupt, numb and spiritually dead the earth will be at that time. It is almost unbelievable to think that after the seven seals, seven trumpets, the destruction from Antichrist, all the killings and the wars, all the famine and the ruins of the environment, there will still be those who do not see the truth!

This will be similar to what God did with Egypt by sending locusts to clean the bark and the fruit off the trees. God killed their cattle and He left them with essentially nothing because He stripped the power so that Pharaoh would let the Israelites go.

This will be the same thing at the end of great tribulation, yet, here they are throwing a party and sending gifts to each other! That shows us how lost this earth will be at that time because they will not recognize or see that God was behind all of these events!

As I've said before, the world will be a very dark place filled with evil but just like the two witnesses God sends, the earth will have a remnant of Believers teaching and preaching the way to salvation. Will you be part of that remnant? What will it take? What will you have to do in order to persevere through it? Stay prepared, alert and ready so that you can be counted faithful at the end.

PERSONAL DEVOTION – DAY 5

TOMORROW'S HEADLINES

READ: DANIEL 11:31-37

We read that strong God-fearing people will distinguish themselves throughout the end times. Some teachings suggest that this group will be taken from the earth in pre-tribulation.

Does this make sense?

Why would God take people that are grounded in their faith from the earth in a time of tribulation? He wouldn't. These people are the ones who will be grounded in a time surrounded by chaos. People will look to them for answers.

These people have a history with God and it means that they have had past victories with God and they understand that prayer works! They know that God is faithful and that deliverance comes even though things look stressful! They know they can trust God because they have a strong history with God!

This is who we want to be. We want to be fortified in our hearts so that when these things begin, no matter where the pattern is or when we are taken out, we know God and we know He is faithful!

The great thing is; God tells us His playbook thousands of years before it happens.

God has said, "I will never leave you or forsake you…" (Hebrews 13:5). God's timing may not be your timing but you can count on Him.

You can be one of the faithful ones. Study and know the Word of the Lord. We have the headlines for tomorrow's newspaper in our hands. God has shown us the events surrounding the seven seals, the seven trumpets and the seven vials. These events are sequential. We can always prepare for what is next.

Take a moment to pray:

"Father, we thank You for this time. Father, we thank You for Your awesome ability to know things before they happen. To know the end from the beginning and as Paul said, 'You knew me before the world was formed.' Your wisdom and Your understanding is beyond human comprehension and we accept Your Word by faith. But You have chosen by revelation, to show us the things that are yet ahead and You have given us a command, not only to know these things ourselves but to teach the next generation so that each generation, after generation, will know Your Word."

SESSION 8
REVELATION 19: THE KING'S RETURN

SESSION 8

REVELATION 19: THE KING'S RETURN

REVELATION 19:7-15

⁷ LET US BE GLAD AND REJOICE AND GIVE HIM GLORY, FOR THE MARRIAGE OF THE LAMB HAS COME, AND HIS WIFE HAS MADE HERSELF READY." ⁸ AND TO HER IT WAS GRANTED TO BE ARRAYED IN FINE LINEN, CLEAN AND BRIGHT, FOR THE FINE LINEN IS THE RIGHTEOUS ACTS OF THE SAINTS. ⁹ THEN HE SAID TO ME, "WRITE: 'BLESSED ARE THOSE WHO ARE CALLED TO THE MARRIAGE SUPPER OF THE LAMB!' " AND HE SAID TO ME, "THESE ARE THE TRUE SAYINGS OF GOD." ¹⁰ AND I FELL AT HIS FEET TO WORSHIP HIM. BUT HE SAID TO ME, "SEE THAT YOU DO NOT DO THAT! I AM YOUR FELLOW SERVANT, AND OF YOUR BRETHREN WHO HAVE THE TESTIMONY OF JESUS. WORSHIP GOD! FOR THE TESTIMONY OF JESUS IS THE SPIRIT OF PROPHECY." ¹¹ NOW I SAW HEAVEN OPENED, AND BEHOLD, A WHITE HORSE. AND HE WHO SAT ON HIM WAS CALLED FAITHFUL AND TRUE, AND IN RIGHTEOUSNESS HE JUDGES AND MAKES WAR. ¹² HIS EYES WERE LIKE A FLAME OF FIRE, AND ON HIS HEAD WERE MANY CROWNS. HE HAD A NAME WRITTEN THAT NO ONE KNEW EXCEPT HIMSELF. ¹³ HE WAS CLOTHED WITH A ROBE DIPPED IN BLOOD, AND HIS NAME IS CALLED THE WORD OF GOD. ¹⁴ AND THE ARMIES IN HEAVEN, CLOTHED IN FINE LINEN, WHITE AND CLEAN, FOLLOWED HIM ON WHITE HORSES. ¹⁵ NOW OUT OF HIS MOUTH GOES A SHARP SWORD, THAT WITH IT HE SHOULD STRIKE THE NATIONS. AND HE HIMSELF WILL RULE THEM WITH A ROD OF IRON. HE HIMSELF TREADS THE WINEPRESS OF THE FIERCENESS AND WRATH OF ALMIGHTY GOD.

---

1. We know what is coming during tribulation because God gave us His _____. We have the _____ for tomorrow's newspaper in our hands. So if we are here during this time, we will know what is coming next.

2. The timing of the Lord's return is only known by _____ _____. When God reveals the Day of the Lord all at once, the mass of people in heaven, the _____, begin praising and worshiping Jesus with great joy and expectation. This is the day Jesus returns to earth for _____ _____.

3. We are looking for this day also, and until then we _____ on the earth and live our lives. We will either meet Jesus at our _____ _____ or in the _____ when those on earth and in heaven are brought together as one complete church.

4. Believers on earth are the _____ of Christ and at the appointed time we become the _____ of Christ at the marriage supper of the Lamb. Essentially, we are engaged to Jesus and our time on earth is spent pursuing a _____ with Him before the spiritual marriage.

5. The Saints in heaven come back with Jesus and they are clothed in clean _____ _____ except for Jesus. His garment is _____ in blood and Jesus will be _____ with scars on His hands, feet, and side for eternity. This will signify for eternity His great sacrifice for mankind.

6. The difference between the _____ Lamb and the _____ Lion should greatly impact us as Christians. The sweet baby Jesus we worship at Christmas will execute the _____ _____ _____ in the end times. He will be like the _____ at His second coming.

7. After the return of Jesus the only two in the _____ _____ _____ will be Antichrist and the False Prophet. The _____ where the lost are sent to the lake of fire is after the _____ reign of Christ which is about one thousand years later.

8. Oftentimes we think of Satan as being in hell but he is not there. He actually goes up into the _____ _____ of God and accuses us before the Throne of God day and night. Only those who died under his _____ and _____ are in hell.

9. At the _____ of the dead we are given different glories, and the difference all _____ on what we do here on earth for the glory of God. Sometimes we have rewards while living, we _____ what we _____, but most of our rewards are yet to come.

10. We are to retain an element of _____ fear when it comes to believing in God. Having righteous fear is having _____ and honor toward God. We are not to be _____ of God but we are to _____ Him as the Father we love with all our heart.

11. While wandering in the desert, the Israelites were fearful of God and they _____ themselves from Him. But Moses did the opposite. He drew _____ to God. Those who are _____ about who God is will back away in fear and never draw close to Him.

12. Jesus told us, "do this in remembrance of Me," so we are to _____ on His return. We must live in _____ waiting for that day. If we are alive, we are not going to _____ great tribulation. Instead we will be prepared, alert and ready, without _____.

KEY WORDS:

(a) Lion of Judah   (b) Body of Christ   (c) Lamb of God   (d) Reverence   (e) Lake of Fire

_____ Title given to Christ in the New Testament with reference to His sacrificial death.

_____ Those who have accepted Jesus Christ as their personal Savior.

_____ Recognizing the authority of God with awe and fear because He is God; adoration.

_____ Conquering King who will slay the enemies of God at His return.

_____ Unsaved are permanently separated from God's love; second death.

SESSION ANSWERS:

1. playbook, headlines
2. Father God, saints, His Bride
3. endure, physical death, rapture
4. Body, Bride, relationship
5. white linen, stained, blemished
6. innocent, roaring, wrath of God, winepress
7. lake of fire, judgment, millennial
8. presence, influence, deception
9. resurrection, depends, reap, sow
10. righteous, respect, frightened, reverence
11. removed, nearer, ignorant
12. focus, anticipation, escape, fear

KEY WORD ANSWERS:

c, b, d, a, e

PERSONAL DEVOTION – DAY 1

LOOK FOR THE DAY

READ: REVELATION 19:1-7

In Mathew 24, we learn that no one knows the day or hour of Christ's return. When the day comes, all of heaven will rejoice. We learned in our study of Daniel that seventy weeks were determined upon his people and the holy city. At the close of the seventieth week, there would be an end to sin and reconciliation for iniquity.

Now, if we understand the time that we are in, then when we see an event happening we will be able to correlate it with whatever is going to happen next. This is similar to what happened with Moses because he had a revelation from God concerning what was going to happen next, and then, he would tell the others and they were able to prepare for their circumstances.

Chapter 19 in the Book of Revelation is dedicated entirely to His return.

We see in, Verse 1, there is great joy and expectation and there is great excitement because at last, Jesus is going to return to the earth!

In Verses 6 and 7, we see there is a clamor of voices going back and forth in heaven, and God gives us a revelation that all the Saints in heaven are shouting because the time has come for the books to be reconciled and God's judgment is here!

Meanwhile, we endure in the earth or we go to meet Him because of physical death, either way we too should look for this day! Not only is this the day that we meet Him, but the whole Church is brought together, to watch Him take His rightful place as King of kings!

At His first coming, He came as a baby in a manger. At His second coming, He will come riding as a victorious King to take what is His.

PERSONAL DEVOTION – DAY 2

A STAINED GARMENT

READ: REVELATION 19:10-21

In Revelation 19:11, we read that the heavens open and a white horse emerges. Jesus, sitting on the white horse, is prepared to judge both the living and the dead.

We see that the eyes of Jesus are a flame of fire, meaning, He is entirely focused on His return and judgment.

I want you to think for a moment about Jesus and how ready He is for this day because the Bible says that He does not even know the day or the hour. He's more excited than we are to spend eternity together!

He is set to make war, to judge and to have this marriage.

We see that Jesus has a name; The Word of God. The Bible tells us, "And the Word became flesh, and dwelt among us..." (John 1:15). And, we read that Jesus has many crowns.

The Believers are dressed in clean white linen and are following Jesus.

For now, no matter where you are regarding the timing of the rapture, it is important to know that these are the Saints who have been separated from their physical bodies. They are coming back with Jesus and they are all clothed in clean white linen, but Jesus is not clothed in clean white linen because His garment is stained with the blood of sinners slain in judgment.

The Savior King. God the Judge.

When you step back to look at this, of all the resurrected bodies in heaven, Jesus is going to be the only One with a blemish.

Jesus will be blemished and He will be the One with the scars on His hands and feet and the whole in His side for eternity and this will signify what He did for us.

PERSONAL DEVOTION – DAY 3

THE LION COMES

READ: REVELATION 19:15-21 // ISAIAH 63:1-7

In these verses we see a much different picture of Jesus than what we normally see throughout the Bible. He is not "sweet baby Jesus." He is bringing judgment and He is completely engaged. He is executing wrath and destroying those who do not walk in love toward Him. This emphasizes the importance of salvation and how significant it is to understand that our salvation is a daily relationship not a one-time experience.

The Bible says that if we do not believe in Him we are condemned already and the wrath of God abides on us. This is the time when all of humanity is judged. Of the seven billion people on the face of the earth, only a very small percentage really knows Jesus Christ as their Lord and Savior.

The Bible tells us that first comes the wrath of God, then the anger of God, and then, the judgment of God.

The wrath of God is poured out during tribulation. The anger of God is seen when Jesus returns and annihilates those who oppose Him. The judgment of God comes after the millennial reign of Christ, a thousand years after His return.

The beast, Antichrist and the False Prophet, are cast alive into the lake of fire immediately following Christ's return at the end of tribulation. Look closely at this timing. They are the only ones in the lake of fire; everyone else who is unsaved is in a place called hell. Once Christ returns, He is going to establish His Kingdom here on earth for one thousand years. After the one thousand years, the final judgment happens. This is the end of all things.

Satan is judged first and thrown into the lake of fire with Antichrist and the False Prophet. Then those who did not make Christ their Lord and Savior will be taken out of hell and cast into the lake of fire.

Believers in Christ experience a completely different type of judgment and live with Christ forever and ever.

It is exciting to think of the day when our Lord returns and brings His Kingdom to this world. As Believers, we will escape eternal death and rule and reign with Christ throughout eternity!

SESSION 8 – DAY 4

THE SALVATION PROCESS

READ: 1 CORINTHIANS 15:40-57

Believe it or not, trumpets are quite divisive in end times study. Some people argue that the trumpet in, 1 Corinthians 15, is a trumpet before the tribulation begins, and then, there are seven more trumpets of judgment in tribulation.

It's pretty clear to me that the trumpet referred to here is the last trumpet. Meaning, there are no more trumpets afterward. This means it must come after the trumpets of judgment. The last trumpet is indeed the last trumpet.

As the last trumpet sounds, the Believers who are dead rise from the dead and the Believers which are alive are caught up together with them. The return of Jesus at the end of tribulation correlates exactly with the rapture of the Church. These events are simultaneous.

According to Scripture, when Jesus was crucified He paid for all three parts of fallen humanity; spirit, soul and body. The Bible says, when Jesus died He went into the earth, into hell, just as anyone else who died would have gone. When He rose again, He rose in spirit and God gave Him a new resurrection body. His resurrection redeemed us spirit, soul and body.

As Believers, the Bible says our spirits are born again at the time of salvation. We become a "new creation." As we go through life, the knowledge of God and His Word renews our mind and we experience salvation in our soul.

When we physically die, our spirit and soul go to heaven. Our mind, our will, our intellect, and our soul will also go with us into heaven. In heaven, what is absent and what still remains of our salvation is our new body. This is the final component of salvation.

It is at the resurrection of the dead and the return of Jesus Christ, along with the rapture of the Church, that our salvation will be complete. We will receive a new immortal body.

Right now those Saints who have died before us do not have a resurrection body.

When Jesus comes back, both alive and dead Believers will be caught up in the air with Him and we will receive our resurrection bodies. This experience will complete the salvation process; spirit, soul and body.

PERSONAL DEVOTION – DAY 5

FEAR OF THE LORD

READ: 1 PETER 1:5-9

When we study the Bible we have to understand the soberness of the return of Jesus Christ. We should have a righteous fear when it comes to believing in God. It's important to understand that living a care-free life and doing whatever you want is not a godly life. We must have an element of respect and an element of honor and an element of fear toward God.

Not to be frightened of God, but reverence Him as God the Father, the Judge and the King of kings. Our desire should be to please Him.

This is the attitude that we must have today and not an attitude that we can just do whatever pleases us.

Remember the parable of the man with the talents.

The man with one talent hid his talent in the earth and he did not work or do anything for the Lord because he was frightened of God. That's not the right attitude. We must fear God in a way that looks to please Him.

It is a type of fear that you would show out of love to your father or your parents. This is the fear that God is looking for in His children.

We must live our life waiting for His return as we look for Him.

Listen to me Saints; we are not going to escape great tribulation because we are going to go through it! We are going to go through great tribulation without fear of man, but with reverence and respect to honor God through all things!

SESSION 9
THE JUDGMENTS OF GOD

SESSION 9
THE JUDGMENTS OF GOD

REVELATION 20:6-15

⁶ BLESSED AND HOLY IS HE WHO HAS PART IN THE FIRST RESURRECTION. OVER SUCH THE SECOND DEATH HAS NO POWER, BUT THEY SHALL BE PRIESTS OF GOD AND OF CHRIST, AND SHALL REIGN WITH HIM A THOUSAND YEARS. ⁷ NOW WHEN THE THOUSAND YEARS HAVE EXPIRED, SATAN WILL BE RELEASED FROM HIS PRISON ⁸ AND WILL GO OUT TO DECEIVE THE NATIONS WHICH ARE IN THE FOUR CORNERS OF THE EARTH, GOG AND MAGOG, TO GATHER THEM TOGETHER TO BATTLE, WHOSE NUMBER IS AS THE SAND OF THE SEA. ⁹ THEY WENT UP ON THE BREADTH OF THE EARTH AND SURROUNDED THE CAMP OF THE SAINTS AND THE BELOVED CITY. AND FIRE CAME DOWN FROM GOD OUT OF HEAVEN AND DEVOURED THEM. ¹⁰ THE DEVIL, WHO DECEIVED THEM, WAS CAST INTO THE LAKE OF FIRE AND BRIMSTONE WHERE THE BEAST AND THE FALSE PROPHET ARE. AND THEY WILL BE TORMENTED DAY AND NIGHT FOREVER AND EVER. ¹¹ THEN I SAW A GREAT WHITE THRONE AND HIM WHO SAT ON IT, FROM WHOSE FACE THE EARTH AND THE HEAVEN FLED AWAY. AND THERE WAS FOUND NO PLACE FOR THEM. ¹² AND I SAW THE DEAD, SMALL AND GREAT, STANDING BEFORE GOD, AND BOOKS WERE OPENED. AND ANOTHER BOOK WAS OPENED, WHICH IS THE BOOK OF LIFE. AND THE DEAD WERE JUDGED ACCORDING TO THEIR WORKS, BY THE THINGS WHICH WERE WRITTEN IN THE BOOKS. ¹³ THE SEA GAVE UP THE DEAD WHO WERE IN IT, AND DEATH AND HADES DELIVERED UP THE DEAD WHO WERE IN THEM. AND THEY WERE JUDGED, EACH ONE ACCORDING TO HIS WORKS. ¹⁴ THEN DEATH AND HADES WERE CAST INTO THE LAKE OF FIRE. THIS IS THE SECOND DEATH. ¹⁵ AND ANYONE NOT FOUND WRITTEN IN THE BOOK OF LIFE WAS CAST INTO THE LAKE OF FIRE.

1. It is important for us to be prepared for _____ _____. We cannot _____ that Christians will escape things, because if we don't escape and we are not prepared, then we will not be able to help others during this great time of _____.

2. Those who died without knowing Jesus Christ are spiritually dead and their names are not in the _____ _____ _____. They did not find salvation and they will be judged based on their works here on earth. There are different _____ in heaven and there will be different levels of _____ in hell.

3. Jesus will rule and reign for a thousand years on earth. This is called the _____ reign of Christ. During this time, Satan will be _____ once more and he will have the ability to _____ some who are alive on earth at this time.

4. After the thousand years, Satan will be _____ and cast into the lake of fire along with all of his _____, the false prophet, and Antichrist. They will remain there in torment for _____.

5. In the middle of the earth there is a place called _____. This place of torment is where the _____ go immediately after their physical death. After the millennium reign of Christ they will be judged according to their works while on earth and then cast into the _____ _____ _____.

6. In the story of the rich man and Lazarus, we learn they both continued to _____ after their life on earth was over. The fate of the rich man was _____ upon his death. To this day, he is still in the _____ _____ _____ and his ultimate fate will be from that place into the lake of fire.

7. When we experience physical death we do not go off into some _____ without our senses. We have the appearance of who we are as a _____ _____ with our soul. Remember, the rich man had his _____ and faculties about him because he tried to negotiate freedom for his brothers.

8. Knowing the ultimate fate of the _____ should set the stage for us and compel us to move forward in _____ the Gospel to those we love. As believers, we are _____ to have the Bible and understand who we are in Christ and where we will spend eternity.

9. The Bible tells us there are levels of judgment. Those who reject the Gospel message and deny the _____ power of God will face a _____ judgment. Their judgment is based on the amount of _____ they should have obtained while listening to the teachings of others.

10. The judgment of Christians is a _____ based on what we did for the glory of God while living. Those who go through life doing righteous acts with the _____ _____ or not done in _____, their acts were done in vain.

11. As believers, we understand that _____ paid for our sins and we have _____ going to hell and into the lake of fire. Sadly, most of the seven billion people on earth are _____ and headed for that place.

12. We must stand between the lost and the lake of fire because God uses us as His _____. We are to show the love of Christ to others and the strength that we have as _____ _____ of the Most High God. We are not to be _____. We are to glorify God with our faith in action.

KEY WORDS:

(a) Rewards   (b) White Throne Judgment   (c) Parable   (d) Torment   (e) Book of Life

_____ Contains the names of those who have been redeemed by the blood of Jesus.

_____ Narrative drawn from nature or human circumstances set forth as a spiritual lesson.

_____ Offered by God to a Believer on the basis of faithful service after salvation.

_____ Final judgment from Jesus Christ prior to the unsaved being cast into the lake of fire.

_____ Utmost degree of misery in mind and body resulting in eternal separation of God.

SESSION ANSWERS:

1. great tribulation, believe, deception
2. book of life, rewards, judgment
3. millennial, released, deceive
4. bound, angels, eternity
5. hell, unsaved, lake of fire
6. exist, sealed, place of torment
7. void, spirit being, memory
8. unsaved, preaching, privileged
9. evident, harsher, revelation
10. reward, wrong heart, love
11. Jesus, escaped, unsaved
12. instruments, obedient servants, mediocre

KEY WORD ANSWERS:

e, c, a, b, d

PERSONAL DEVOTION – DAY 1

REQUEST DENIED

READ: REVELATION 20 // LUKE 16

Revelation 20 talks about the judgments of God. The first thing I want you to notice is in, Verse 12, where we read the word *book* and this book refers to the Book of Life. There are different rewards in heaven and there will be different levels of judgment in hell.

In Verse 13, we see another word that is plural and that word is *works*. Those who are spiritually dead are not in the Book of Life. The spiritually dead are those who didn't find salvation and they will be judged based on their works here on the earth.

Jesus tells a story of a wealthy man and a beggar named Lazarus in, Luke 16. Now, because of the way Jesus sets the story up, we have reason to believe these two people actually existed. So, this is not a parable.

When both of these men died, the rich man probably had a lot of people at his funeral with a lot of flowers, and perhaps some dignitaries in attendance. On the other side of the tracks, the poor man, Lazarus, probably had a pine box and a state arranged funeral with a handful of people.

Here on earth both of these men died physically, yet, the Bible tells us that they did not cease to exist.

We learn from Scripture that they have now gone into two separate places in eternity. The rich man went to a place called hell, and Lazarus went to another place called Abraham's Bosom, a place of comfort for Believers.

The rich man said, "I am in torment. Have Lazarus, the guy who ate out of my garbage can on earth, dip the tips of his fingers in water to give me some drink." But Abraham tells him, "No one can pass between the two places."

When we die physically we do not go off into some void without our senses. We still have the appearance of who we are as a spirit being with our soul. This rich man still had his memory, he still had his faculties about him, and he was still able to negotiate for water. He also had enough capacity to say, "Listen, I do not want my five brothers to come to this place." He begged Abraham to go and tell them about this place of torment and the agony therein because he did not want them to experience anything like it.

Abraham denied his request, and said if they did not believe the Word of God then they are not going to believe in a miracle.

The rich man sealed his fate here on earth. Also, I want you to know that the rich man is still there today in the place of torment! His ultimate fate will be from hell into the lake of fire. As Believers, we can look forward to living eternally with Christ here on earth!

PERSONAL DEVOTION – DAY 2

EVERYONE GOES SOMEWHERE

READ: ISAIAH 14:9-11

This is probably one of the more interesting passages of imagery that we have in the Bible about looking into hell.

Verse 9, tells us that, "Hell has moved to meet thee at thy coming..." Picture a door in hell and everyone there has his or her eyes fixed on the door. They are anticipating who is coming in next to join them. The Bible tells us that the kings of the earth, and people of great influence and wealth will be notable, and those who are in hell will recognize who they are.

Can you imagine the anticipation and the dread? The hopelessness these souls must feel as, captains of industry or political figures or famous athletes, when they enter into torment forever. It's very scary.

We learn in, Verse 11, that in hell, "...the worms will cover thee and the worms will be under thee."

Most of us do not understand what this means, because we don't know about ancient forms of torture. Just outside the city gates they would stretch out your arms and legs and tie them to the ground, and then, over the next several blistering hot days you would be eaten alive by the insects, the scorpions and the wild animals.

Needless to say, this would be a very slow and extremely torturous way to die but this is the description of, "the worms will cover thee and the worms will be under thee."

I probably just spoiled your breakfast, but hold on, there is good news!

We see here in Scripture that when Believers die we do go somewhere else. Praise God!

We get to experience streets of gold, rivers of life and most of all the presence of God! Everyone will go somewhere and we, as Believers, are privileged to have the Bible and an understanding of who we are in Christ.

This is just another reason why we are to be thankful that we have the Word of God and that we know His Son, Jesus Christ.

PERSONAL DEVOTION – DAY 3

A HARSHER JUDGMENT

READ: MATTHEW 11 AND 12

In Matthew 11, Jesus is talking about John the Baptist. He poses an interesting question, He asks, "What did they expect to see when they went out into the wilderness? Did they expect to see a man dressed in a great fashionable suit and well groomed?"

John was a Nazarite, which means he never cut his hair and he had an unruly beard, and he followed a certain diet of locust and honey. According to Jesus, this is God's greatest man.

He tells them that John preached the Word, but there was no reaction. They were dull to the truth and unmoved by the Word of God.

I want you to see where Jesus is going with this analogy because He continues with it in the next verses.

Jesus is saying that because you were presented with a strong message, and that the power of God was very evident amongst you, and you had this revelation that you could have seen but you did not see, and because you were given much, consequently, your judgment is going to be harsher than the judgment of others.

Do you see the levels of judgment here? You are not judged based on your works only. Your judgment also includes the amount of revelation and wisdom that you should have obtained.

The Bible tells us to go into the entire world and preach the Gospel, right?

We learn in, Luke 12:46, that the man who says in his heart that the Lord delays His coming will be appointed his portion with the unbelievers. This means, he was a Believer but he lived worldly and now he is appointed with the unbelievers. This is the punishment deserving of an unbeliever.

Today, check your heart. Take inventory of the wisdom and the preaching you have heard. You are responsible to God for that truth.

PERSONAL DEVOTION – DAY 4

EXAMINE YOUR MOTIVES

READ: 2 PETER 2:20-21 // 1 CORINTHIANS 3:10-16

Hebrews 10:29 says, "A sorer punishment, supposed he that trodden foot the Son of God and His blood where with he was once sanctified."

This verse tells us that where you have a revelation than you also have a responsibility. Therefore, it is critical that you understand the judgments of God.

Alright, this now leaves the Believers. What is going to happen to us? To some degree this is more important because it is personal, right?

The foundation of our life is in believing that Jesus Christ is our Lord and Savior. We build upon the foundation of believing in Jesus Christ through gold, silver, precious stones, wood, hay, and stubble.

The Bible refers to these as works in, 1 Corinthians 3:12.

Allow me to first create an image in your mind of what this means. One day, you will stand alone, before God to be judged. Your actions, words and faith, will be laid out before you. These things are represented by gold, silver, precious stone, wood, hay, and stubble.

This is the pile before you in judgment and fire comes down and burns up the wood, hay and stubble leaving only the gold, silver and precious stone which are the things of enduring value.

Now, our judgment is not about us paying for our sins, because our sins have already been paid for by the death, burial and resurrection of Jesus Christ.

We get rewarded for what we do because our sins were dealt with through Jesus Christ.

The wood, hay and stubble are righteous acts done with the wrong heart. They are righteous acts that you think you deserve a reward for, but they were done with the wrong heart. Please read Mathew 6 regarding prayer, giving and fasting.

Today, ask yourself, am I doing things for the right reasons? Are my actions for myself or for the Kingdom of God?

PERSONAL DEVOTION – DAY 5

LOVE IS EVERYTHING

READ: 1 CORINTHIANS 13

Love is the only thing that matters. This sounds like a Beatles song, but the Bible says, "If you have not agape love, charity, your works profit you nothing!" We are called to give, to pray, and to fast, but if you do not walk in love than there is no eternal value.

Stop and think about that for a moment. If you are all-in with your life but not walking in love, then what does it matter?

Just as, we measure a child by marking the wall with a little line as they grow taller and taller, our height in Christianity is not measured based on the fact that we can teach the Word or we can quote Scriptures or that we know the Greek or the Hebrew. Our height in Christianity is measured by how much love we walk in.

There is the economy of the world that says, "I need your glory and I need to feed off your glory." Then there is the economy of heaven that says, "I just need God to see it, because in His eyes it has the greatest value."

We are not judged by our actions, but judged based on our righteous actions that we do in love. I want you to know this, because as Believers we do not receive a judgment that would bring us pain.

We are to show the love, the faith and the strength that we have, so that as obedient servants of the Most High God, we live a life that is pleasing to Him.

Remember, to the world John the Baptist looked like he was a big loser because he did not have a home, his appearance was offensive, and more than likely, you would not want to sit next to him in Church.

SESSION 10

THE CHURCH, THE FALSE CHURCH AND JUDGMENT

SESSION 10

THE CHURCH, THE FALSE CHURCH AND JUDGMENT

MATTHEW 25:1-13

¹ "THEN THE KINGDOM OF HEAVEN SHALL BE LIKENED TO TEN VIRGINS WHO TOOK THEIR LAMPS AND WENT OUT TO MEET THE BRIDEGROOM. ² NOW FIVE OF THEM WERE WISE, AND FIVE WERE FOOLISH. ³ THOSE WHO WERE FOOLISH TOOK THEIR LAMPS AND TOOK NO OIL WITH THEM, ⁴ BUT THE WISE TOOK OIL IN THEIR VESSELS WITH THEIR LAMPS. ⁵ BUT WHILE THE BRIDEGROOM WAS DELAYED, THEY ALL SLUMBERED AND SLEPT. ⁶ AND AT MIDNIGHT A CRY WAS HEARD: 'BEHOLD, THE BRIDEGROOM IS COMING; GO OUT TO MEET HIM!' ⁷ THEN ALL THOSE VIRGINS AROSE AND TRIMMED THEIR LAMPS. ⁸ AND THE FOOLISH SAID TO THE WISE, 'GIVE US SOME OF YOUR OIL, FOR OUR LAMPS ARE GOING OUT.' ⁹ BUT THE WISE ANSWERED, SAYING, 'NO, LEST THERE SHOULD NOT BE ENOUGH FOR US AND YOU; BUT GO RATHER TO THOSE WHO SELL, AND BUY FOR YOURSELVES.' ¹⁰ AND WHILE THEY WENT TO BUY, THE BRIDEGROOM CAME, AND THOSE WHO WERE READY WENT IN WITH HIM TO THE WEDDING; AND THE DOOR WAS SHUT. ¹¹ AFTERWARD THE OTHER VIRGINS CAME ALSO, SAYING, 'LORD, LORD, OPEN TO US!' ¹² BUT HE ANSWERED AND SAID, 'ASSUREDLY, I SAY TO YOU, I DO NOT KNOW YOU.' ¹³ WATCH THEREFORE, FOR YOU KNOW NEITHER THE DAY NOR THE HOUR IN WHICH THE SON OF MAN IS COMING.

---

1. When Jesus returns He is going to _____ the books and He will divide all of humanity into two _____. There will be those who _____ to the sound of His voice and those who went about living their lives with no regard to His Word.

2. Noah had a _____ from God and he began to prepare himself and his family. He organized his days in order to be ready for what God had spoken to him while the rest of humanity went about their _____ _____. People looked at Noah and the ark as _____.

3. When the rain washed over the land, Noah was _____ in the ark with his family. Noah harkened unto the _____ ____ _____ and that was the difference between those who _____ and Noah's family. When Jesus returns it is going to be too late for many people.

4. Jesus clearly gives us many _____ signs before His return in the Bible. The book of Revelation lays out in great _____ what is going to happen at the end time. Those who own a Bible have no _____ but to prepare themselves and their families just as Noah did.

5. People who have the _____ to hear and know the Word of God to prepare for His return but do nothing are self-identified Christians. This is the _____ _____ Jesus speaks about when He returns to the earth. Jesus expects us to be actively _____ Him at all times.

6. They Holy Spirit cautions us to be very sensitive of the time we are living in because we do not know the _____ or the _____. As faithful and wise servants we are to be _____ for our Master's return and doing His work. We must not be caught _____.

7. Jesus is not looking for lukewarm, _____-_____, so-called believers. When we truly understand what Jesus did for us and the results of His _____, there is no other way for us to live other than to be all-in for Him. Knowing this in your heart is true _____.

8. After the _____ ____ _____, a group of believers began to praise the risen Lord and they were filled again with the Holy Ghost. Likewise, we must _____ ourselves with the Spirit of the Lord continuously. We cannot allow our supply of oil, the _____, run dry in our lives.

9. It is our _____ engagement with the Lord that fills us over and over again with His oil. We are to be re-filled _____ with the Holy Spirit because, what would happen if we never _____ or _____ Him again in our lives?

10. There is an _____ of Jesus in wanting His people to love Him with all our hearts and to be _____ with Him every day. Jesus wants His followers to be filled to _____, to live for Him and be with Him always, just as He is always with us.

11. God _____ us with talents while here on earth and we are called to use these talents to _____ the body of Christ. Remember, Jesus taught us that He will cut the _____ branches off the vine and toss them away. Clearly we have a _____ upon us from Jesus to be fruitful.

12. The Word is the _____ that comes into our hearts and minds when we hear His teachings. The _____ is our obedience and the outward _____ of the Word within us. The fruit of the Spirit are Christ-like _____ that others should readily see in our lives.

KEY WORDS:

(a) Manifestation   (b) Empowerment   (c) Pentecost   (d) Half-Hearted   (e) Hypocrisy

_____ Celebrates the descent of the Holy Spirit upon the followers of Jesus Christ.

_____ Enlightenment about God; making Him known or revelation of Him.

_____ Authority or power given by God to someone in order to do His will.

_____ Assuming a false appearance of virtue and beliefs; deceitful show of good character.

_____ Doing things without real effort, enthusiasm or belief in the outcome.

SESSION ANSWERS:

1. reconcile, categories, harkened
2. revelation, daily routine, foolishness
3. enclosed, voice of God, perished
4. warning, detail, excuse
5. capacity, false church, serving
6. day, hour, watching, unaware
7. half-hearted, sacrifice, salvation
8. Day of Pentecost, replenish, anointing
9. perpetual, daily, praised, worshiped
10. expectation engaged, capacity
11. entrusted, multiply, unfruitful, demand
12. seed, fruit, manifestation, characteristics

KEY WORD ANSWERS:

c, a, b, e, d

PERSONAL DEVOTION – DAY 1

NO ORDINARY DAY

READ: MATTHEW 24:35-42

Jesus gives us six parables that relate to His return. They describe how we will be judged in His eyes.

In Matthew 24:35-42, we are told the angels do not know when Jesus is coming back. We looked at this earlier in our study and when Jesus opens with the parallel of the end times in these verses, He is comparing it to the days of Noah. He was talking about being prepared, alert and ready. Jesus describes how Noah had a revelation of what God was going to do, so he began to prepare himself and his family.

The Bible tells us that before the flood, before the judgment, before the action that God spoke of, and before the revelation came to manifestation, all of humanity was going about living their life. In other words, they were doing what ordinary humans do every single day.

They were getting up and going to work as a carpenter, a lawyer, a doctor, or whatever they may have been. Jesus says that His return is going to be just like the days of Noah. And, this is a very good example for us, because Noah was preparing.

Consider what it was like to be a human listening to one of Noah's sermons that the flood is coming. They were probably skeptical.

Then, all of a sudden one day it starts raining and the water starts moving quickly and it gets higher, and higher, and higher! It passes over your knees, it reaches your waist, and then, it touches your shoulders and you watch as it covers over the land and starts rising up to the trees. Then, you turn around and look for Noah but he is shut up in the ark and protected because he harkened unto the voice of God! That was the difference between those that perished and those that lived in the days of Noah.

Jesus clearly spoke of the signs and what you can look for before His return, but not only that, He gave us a whole book – the Book of Revelation, that lays out in great detail as to what is going to happen at the end of time. Believers have no excuse but to prepare ourselves for the return of the Lord.

PERSONAL DEVOTION – DAY 2

ALL-IN FOR JESUS

READ: MATTHEW 24:42-51

Let's say you live on a street and there are homes on both sides and three or four of your neighbors homes were broken into. You look down the street and you realize that first it was Bill's house that was broken into. Next, it was Don's house that was broken into, and then, it was Betty's house that was broken into. In all cases, somebody broke into the garage, and then, got into their house when they were not home. Well, with this information you would know that there is a thief in the neighborhood, right?

You would be very sensitive to what is going on and you would be very alert to strangers. And, before you went to bed you would make sure that your dwelling was secure against the thief.

Well, this is what the Holy Spirit is trying to convey to us in, Matthew 24. We need to be sensitive and ready all the time, because His return can happen at any time.

In Matthew 24:44, the Bible tells us, "Therefore you also be ready for in such an hour as you think not the Son of man cometh." Now, one of the things He is telling us to do is to be ready. The action words in these verses are; be watching, be ready, be faithful, be wise, and be doing! I want you to have the feeling of always being alert and ready.

In the parable of the servant and the master, Jesus is not speaking about an unbeliever because this is somebody who knows Him as Lord. In Verse 48, the evil servant calls Jesus, "...my Lord."

The word I want you to learn in today's teaching is *conditional*. In the parables of, Matthew 24 and 25, I want you to see who is doing the Word of God, and who is obeying the Word of God.

We read in, Verse 48, this servant said, "...My Lord is not here." He felt he could live any way he wanted to live and not obey the Word of God.

But, what was the response from Jesus, "You were caught unaware and you were not doing what I told you to do. Yet, you had the capacity to know and you should have known. Even still, you have made the decision not to follow My Word."

Essentially Jesus wants us all-in. He does not want half or three-quarters of us. He does not want small fragments or pieces of us. Jesus expects us to be all-in for Him just as He was all-in for us!

That is His expectation of His followers. Jesus is not looking for somebody who is an occasional lukewarm, half-hearted, so-called Believer; because if you truly understand what He did for you, and the results of His actions, then there would be no other way you could live other than to be all-in for Jesus.

PERSONAL DEVOTION – DAY 3

CHECK YOUR OIL

READ: MATTHEW 25:1-13

The ten virgins are all Christians, and they are all waiting for the return of Jesus. In Scripture, *oil* has always represented a type of anointing.

Jesus uses this as an example to show that the virgins all had the capacity to fill their lamps and to be ready to bring light to the Bridegroom. This was their focus in life.

The Bible tells us, five of them were foolish because they were not ready and they had no oil, no anointing, even though they had the capacity for the anointing.

The other five had oil so they were able to bring light. They were prepared, alert and ready.

Jesus answered and said to the five who were foolish, "I do not have a relationship with you and you are not coming with Me."

What is Jesus talking about here? What did these five virgins do that was so foolish?

How do we make sure we have oil in our lamps?

These five virgins did not have the anointing and it is our continual interaction with the Lord that fills us up again with Spiritual oil. You see, the anointing is something that comes upon us but we should regularly, daily, engage with God and continue to be filled with His Spirit.

I want to encourage you not to become like the foolish virgins that were not ready because they were not engaged with the One who loved them and the One that they should have loved in return. There is an expectation of Jesus wanting His followers to love Him with all their heart and to be engaged with Him every day.

PERSONAL DEVOTION – DAY 4
MULTIPLY YOUR TALENTS

READ: MATTHEW 25:14-23

In this parable of the talents, the Lord called His own servants and gave them something. He gave them the amount that they were able to handle. He was not unrighteous or unfair in the distribution of talents. He took something that was His possession and He empowered it into the hands of someone who had a relationship with Him. The key is; they all ready had a relationship with the Lord. These are Christians.

Jesus gave all of us something that we should use to produce something greater. God expects us to take our natural abilities, our super-natural abilities and the resources we have to enhance and grow the Kingdom of God.

We are called to increase the body of Christ and we are called to supply the body of Christ. We are called to take what we have and impart it to one another.

In the Book of John, Jesus taught us that we must be fruitful and bear fruit. Then, what did Jesus do with the unfruitful ones? He cut the branches off from the vine and He tossed them away.

The fruit is obedience to the Word of God, because the Word is the seed that comes into our hearts and minds. The fruit is the outward manifestation of the Word of God within our heart.

In Galatians 5:22-23, we learn the fruit is; love, joy, peace, long suffering, gentleness, kindness, and meekness. It is the Word operating and functioning in our heart which is the seed that is planted in us. When those newly planted seeds grow they will manifest and reveal the Word of God in your life.

Jesus punished the evil servant because he was unfruitful. He was lazy; he did not truly know God. This man produced nothing with his life, and therefore, what was his ultimate fate? He was cast into hell.

Today, be encouraged, go out and use your talents and resources to grow and expand the Kingdom of God.

PERSONAL DEVOTION – DAY 5
ACQUIRE OR GIVE?

READ: JAMES 1:26-27 // JAMES 2:14-18

James is talking about salvation and faith. Our actions cement our salvation.

The economy of heaven is the complete opposite of the economy of earth because on earth you build a fortune; you build a bigger house, have a nicer car, and put your kids through private school. It's all about building yourself up. It's all about acquiring.

In the economy of heaven, it's not about acquiring, but about giving. It's all about giving your time, your money and your resources. It's all about sacrifice and faith.

Jesus wants us to show Him that we have faith! You think you have faith and you believe in Me, than show Me! That is the difference between the true Church and those that are just self-identified church-goers. Jesus is looking for those who are sold out for Him and willing to sell everything to follow Him.

Today, there are people in your city who are starving and homeless. In fact, I bet you could find someone to fit this description just a few miles from where you are right now! Jesus is saying that instead of acquiring more food and more possessions – you should give to others.

Let your light shine in your city. Produce fruit of good works and sacrifice.

SESSION 11
THE SNARE

SESSION 11
THE SNARE

MATTHEW 23:29-39

²⁹ WOE TO YOU, SCRIBES AND PHARISEES, HYPOCRITES! BECAUSE YOU BUILD THE TOMBS OF THE PROPHETS AND ADORN THE MONUMENTS OF THE RIGHTEOUS, ³⁰ AND SAY, 'IF WE HAD LIVED IN THE DAYS OF OUR FATHERS, WE WOULD NOT HAVE BEEN PARTAKERS WITH THEM IN THE BLOOD OF THE PROPHETS.' ³¹ THEREFORE YOU ARE WITNESSES AGAINST YOURSELVES THAT YOU ARE SONS OF THOSE WHO MURDERED THE PROPHETS. ³² FILL UP, THEN, THE MEASURE OF YOUR FATHERS' GUILT. ³³ SERPENTS, BROOD OF VIPERS! HOW CAN YOU ESCAPE THE CONDEMNATION OF HELL? ³⁴ THEREFORE, INDEED, I SEND YOU PROPHETS, WISE MEN, AND SCRIBES: SOME OF THEM YOU WILL KILL AND CRUCIFY, AND SOME OF THEM YOU WILL SCOURGE IN YOUR SYNAGOGUES AND PERSECUTE FROM CITY TO CITY, ³⁵ THAT ON YOU MAY COME ALL THE RIGHTEOUS BLOOD SHED ON THE EARTH, FROM THE BLOOD OF RIGHTEOUS ABEL TO THE BLOOD OF ZECHARIAH, SON OF BERECHIAH, WHOM YOU MURDERED BETWEEN THE TEMPLE AND THE ALTAR. ³⁶ ASSUREDLY, I SAY TO YOU, ALL THESE THINGS WILL COME UPON THIS GENERATION ³⁷ "O JERUSALEM, JERUSALEM, THE ONE WHO KILLS THE PROPHETS AND STONES THOSE WHO ARE SENT TO HER! HOW OFTEN I WANTED TO GATHER YOUR CHILDREN TOGETHER, AS A HEN GATHERS HER CHICKS UNDER HER WINGS, BUT YOU WERE NOT WILLING! ³⁸ SEE! YOUR HOUSE IS LEFT TO YOU DESOLATE ³⁹ FOR I SAY TO YOU, YOU SHALL SEE ME NO MORE TILL YOU SAY, 'BLESSED IS HE WHO COMES IN THE NAME OF THE LORD!' "

---

1. The _____ _____ represents Israel, and Jesus told us to behold the fig tree so we can interpret this to be the nation of Israel. We can understand Scripture to indicate when _____ is tender and young, _____, and being fruitful, we know that summer is nigh.

2. Israel was _____ from 70 A.D. until 1948, when it became a nation even though its borders were not complete until 1967. This is when Israel took back the _____ _____ which included Jerusalem. Now, Jerusalem is back in the _____ of Israel.

3. The _____ that saw Israel come back together and the _____ given to us from Jesus lead us to conclude we are living in that season. The return of Jesus could not have taken place prior to _____ because the temple was not built, but the _____ is set for the return of the Lord.

4. Jerusalem is the center of Biblical _____, and when we see the city _____ about with _____, we know the desolation is near. Essentially, the generation that witnessed the return of Jerusalem to Israel is the time period we stand in today. Saints, we are that generation.

5. Our senses are continuously engaged today with modern _____. We look to be _____ and informed with the latest updates on current events, weather, sports, and even personal relationships. We are overcharged and _____ with the cares of this life.

6. Jesus told us the snare of being _____ and too busy was coming on the earth to all of _____. He warned us that the busyness of this world will cause some of us to miss the day of His return. The day will come upon us and some will be _____.

7. When we _____ participate in the social needs and energies of the world, we must be alert to our _____ because we can be caught in Satan's trap. Then we begin to lose our _____ and become spiritually dull to the things of God.

8. Technology is changing _____ attendance. Today, we can watch a Sunday service on television or the internet anytime, but we are told not to forsake the _____ of ourselves together. There is a very special _____ when the church comes together as a family.

9. The church is _____ because it is losing the focus of loving your _____ as yourself and loving God with all your heart, mind and soul. Jesus told us the church would drift and turn their ears from the _____ and begin listening to messages that would satisfy itching ears.

10. Remember, Jesus would stop and talk to one _____ person in order to change their life. The traps that we find ourselves in are set deliberately by Satan to satisfy the _____ _____ of the flesh. Satan tries to keep our focus on ourselves so we lose touch with God.

11. On the day of His return, things may not go _____ to your liking and you may have to go _____ what your flesh desires. Prepare yourself ahead of time because the signs Jesus spoke of are happening right now in our _____ and on our watch!

KEY WORDS:

(a) Pursue   (b) Church Age   (c) Snare   (d) Surfeiting   (e) Disperse

_____ Desirable and unsuspecting traps set by Satan; allurements to sin.

_____ Parenthesis or pause in God's dealing with His chosen covenant people.

_____ Excess of things; overindulgence or being overcharged in your senses.

_____ Strive to gain or seek to accomplish something that is likely unattainable.

_____ Drive or send off in various directions; to scatter or remove.

SESSION ANSWERS:

1. fig tree, Jerusalem, budding
2. desolate, West Bank, possession
3. generation, signs, 1967, stage
4. prophecy, encompassed, armies
5. technology, entertained, surfeiting
6. preoccupied, humanity, unaware
7. constantly, circumstances, focus
8. church, assembling, anointing
9. diminishing, neighbor, truth
10. homeless, selfish desires, ourselves
11. according, against, generation

KEY WORD ANSWERS:

c, b, d, a, e

PERSONAL DEVOTION – DAY 1

WATCH THE FIG TREE

READ: MATTHEW 24:29-35

In the Books of Joel and Jeremiah, along with several other places in the Bible, the fig tree is representative of Israel.

In Matthew, Chapters 23 through 25, we read that Jesus is talking about His return and He references the fig tree. When Jesus says, "Watch the fig tree," we can read it to mean, "Watch the nation of Israel and the city of Jerusalem."

Jesus is saying, "When the fig tree, (Jerusalem), is tender and young know that summer is nigh." This is when Jerusalem is beginning to bud or beginning to be fruitful. In the last verse of Matthew 23, Jesus tells us, that Jerusalem would be desolate for a period of time. Jesus also goes on to tell us that Jerusalem would lay waste for a period of time. This happened from 70 A.D. until May 14, 1948, because Israel was not a nation during this time.

The nation of Israel came back together in 1948 and it was a miracle. And then, Israel took back the West Bank, including Jerusalem in 1967. This, to me, is the most significant date, since Jerusalem is God's time-piece.

Jesus told us that the generation who sees Israel come back together as a nation, and to include Jerusalem, would see His return.

Which begs the question: How long is a generation?

When Jesus talks of the fig tree, the time frame is about 30 A.D. Jerusalem was then destroyed in 70 A.D., meaning, what Jesus said took place forty years later.

From the birth of Jesus to the destruction of the Temple was about 70 years.

Could Jesus be giving us a clue of His return in relation to the fig tree?

If so, this is very exciting! And, until that time comes, we should continue to prepare ourselves daily for His return.

PERSONAL DEVOTION – DAY 2

TRACKING YOUR STEPS

READ: REVELATION 13:15-18

Never before in history has there ever been the ability to track every single transaction. Just ten years ago there was not the capability to be completely paperless but now, today, we have this ability.

In fact, society is moving cashless on its own because everyone is moving very slightly over to using debit cards, credit cards and web transactions.

Not only are we becoming accustomed to this technology, but whether we know it or not, all of our motions can be very easily tracked.

You take your cell phone wherever you go and whoever wants to, or has the access to, can look and see where you have been, where you are going, what you are purchasing, and what your habits are. They can easily monitor when you are walking and when you are not walking, when you are active and when you are not active, they can determine what you are doing and when you are doing it. Some of these programs can even tell you how many steps you took throughout the day.

The mark, the number of the beast, never could have existed ten or twenty years ago, but now we are in a period where it's easy to implement. We are being prepared for it right now.

People assume that the mark of the beast will be something very obvious and it will be a new technology or a new system. Stop and think; could this new technology and structure all ready be in place, just not fully enacted?

PERSONAL DEVOTION – DAY 3

CULTIVATE YOUR GARDEN

READ: LUKE 8:10-15

We are supposed to be fruitful in the faith. In previous sessions, we learned that if we are not fruitful and good caretakers of our salvation, we will be cut-off like the evil servant in the parable of the five talents.

In Luke 8 we read, the Word of God comes into a heart, yet it brings no fruit to perfection.

What is Jesus really talking about in these verses?

Jesus is talking about salvation.

He says that the Gospel comes to some, but it is taken by Satan. It cannot grow and the Believer cannot be fruitful, therefore, they cannot be saved. When the Word falls on rocks, it means someone with a hardened heart. The Word was received with joy but the Word did not take root in their life, and then, they cannot be saved.

Then, some people hear the Word and receive it. As it begins to grow, the cares of this life and the deceitfulness of riches, surfeiting and drunkenness, cause the Word to be choked and they become unfruitful.

This is the snare. The trap is busyness and being distracted. Satan will keep us so busy through social needs and social energies that we are unaware and trapped by participating with the world and what they are doing. Suddenly, we will find ourselves losing focus and becoming spiritually dull, and then, ever so slightly falling away.

When a plant grows and is choked by weeds; it is a slow process. This does not happen overnight it happens gradually.

So, Jesus is telling us to take heed that the day does not come upon you unaware, because you can become so spiritually dull that you find yourself in the snare, and then, it will be too late.

Today, be aware of your spiritual development and your spiritual growth. We must continue to make our hearts good and pliable ground for the Word of God.

PERSONAL DEVOTION – DAY 4

DO NOT PURSUE THESE THINGS

READ: GENESIS 3

What did Satan really do with Adam and Eve in the garden when he said, in Genesis 3:4, "…you shall not surely die?" What Satan did was he gave them a false sense of security and he told them there would be no consequences to their actions.

Then what did Eve do? She began to negotiate with her own lust for what she wanted in her life.

This is the same thing in each of our daily lives as Satan presents us with opportunities. Every commercial we watch on television tells us that we are lacking something. We either need more hair or better hair or cleaner and shinier hair or a different color hair!

I'm not calling these commercials satanic. I'm using them as an example of what the Enemy does to us on a spiritual level. It is the same message Satan gives us every day – we are lacking something and because of our lack we are in need; because we are in need then we pursue false truth, false love and false hope. Then we fall into his trap!

Why does this happen?

It happens because it is difficult to just say, *"No!"*

It is difficult to push back from the rest of the herd when they are all running in the same direction.

Today, we should focus on what the truth of God's Word says and hold onto His promises, so that we are not lured out into the snare of the Enemy which is the snare of comparison, the snare of inadequacy and the snare of being better.

PERSONAL DEVOTION – DAY 5

THE CHURCH IS DRIFTING

READ: MATTHEW 24:9-10

The snare Satan presents makes us think only about ourselves and self-preservation. That's exactly what is happening in Matthew 24:9-10.

This means that the sense of duty to the other man in the end times is gone. Everyone is only thinking about themselves and their lives. This is even in the Church!

Now, when you have a Church that is apostate or moving in this direction, than it is a Church that looks like the world and it becomes a selfish Church.

These verses in Matthew tell us that the Church will diminish and melt away because it loses the focus of love.

That trap set by Satan, puts the Church and Believers, in a place where they cannot absorb persecution, but rather react.

Jesus tells us ahead of time that this is where the Church is drifting.

The apostles asked Him what is going to be a sign of Your coming, Jesus answered; "Look at what the Church is doing!" If the Church is not enduring sound doctrine and they are turning their ears away from the truth and they are satisfying an itch with a Gospel that will make them feel comfortable in their current lifestyle, then the end is near!

You must gauge Christianity based on love and hearts that have been changed and based on the work of the ministry!

The traps that we find ourselves in are set for us by the flesh and what the flesh desires. Satan caters to it. The Enemy sets up a structure of keeping us busy, keeping us in lack, keeping us wanting things, keeping us self-centered, and trying to keep up with the rest of the world. All of these things bring us to a place where we do not even know the trouble that is happening around us.

We have to change this, and the only way to change it, is by reading the Word of God.

SESSION 12

WHAT'S NEXT?

SESSION 12
WHAT'S NEXT?

EZEKIEL 37:1-10; 21-22

¹ THE HAND OF THE LORD CAME UPON ME AND BROUGHT ME OUT IN THE SPIRIT OF THE LORD, AND SET ME DOWN IN THE MIDST OF THE VALLEY; AND IT WAS FULL OF BONES. ² THEN HE CAUSED ME TO PASS BY THEM ALL AROUND, AND BEHOLD, THERE WERE VERY MANY IN THE OPEN VALLEY; AND INDEED THEY WERE VERY DRY. ³ AND HE SAID TO ME, "SON OF MAN, CAN THESE BONES LIVE?" SO I ANSWERED, "O LORD GOD, YOU KNOW." ⁴ AGAIN HE SAID TO ME, "PROPHESY TO THESE BONES, AND SAY TO THEM, 'O DRY BONES, HEAR THE WORD OF THE LORD! ⁵ THUS SAYS THE LORD GOD TO THESE BONES: "SURELY I WILL CAUSE BREATH TO ENTER INTO YOU, AND YOU SHALL LIVE. ⁶ I WILL PUT SINEWS ON YOU AND BRING FLESH UPON YOU, COVER YOU WITH SKIN AND PUT BREATH IN YOU; AND YOU SHALL LIVE. THEN YOU SHALL KNOW THAT I AM THE LORD." ⁷ SO I PROPHESIED AS I WAS COMMANDED; AND AS I PROPHESIED, THERE WAS A NOISE, AND SUDDENLY A RATTLING; AND THE BONES CAME TOGETHER, BONE TO BONE. ⁸ INDEED, AS I LOOKED, THE SINEWS AND THE FLESH CAME UPON THEM, AND THE SKIN COVERED THEM OVER; BUT THERE WAS NO BREATH IN THEM. ⁹ ALSO HE SAID TO ME, "PROPHESY TO THE BREATH, PROPHESY, SON OF MAN, AND SAY TO THE BREATH, 'THUS SAYS THE LORD GOD: "COME FROM THE FOUR WINDS, O BREATH, AND BREATHE ON THESE SLAIN, THAT THEY MAY LIVE."' ¹⁰ SO I PROPHESIED AS HE COMMANDED ME, AND BREATH CAME INTO THEM, AND THEY LIVED, AND STOOD UPON THEIR FEET, AN EXCEEDINGLY GREAT ARMY.

²¹ THEN SAY TO THEM, 'THUS SAYS THE LORD GOD: "SURELY I WILL TAKE THE CHILDREN OF ISRAEL FROM AMONG THE NATIONS, WHEREVER THEY HAVE GONE, AND WILL GATHER THEM FROM EVERY SIDE AND BRING THEM INTO THEIR OWN LAND; ²² AND I WILL MAKE THEM ONE NATION IN THE LAND, ON THE MOUNTAINS OF ISRAEL; AND ONE KING SHALL BE KING OVER THEM ALL; THEY SHALL NO LONGER BE TWO NATIONS, NOR SHALL THEY EVER BE DIVIDED INTO TWO KINGDOMS AGAIN.

SESSION 12

1. Thousands of years in advance, _____ wrote that Israel would come together again as a nation. He saw _____ _____ and God told him to speak to the bones and tell them they are going to _____. The bones came together and Israel became a nation in 1948, which is a miracle.

2. We see on television networks how Russian forces have moved onto the _____ of Israel, and we studied about this great _____ in the book of Ezekiel. The enemies of Israel are advancing toward this war and the _____ behind their movement is wealth, great wealth.

3. One of the largest _____ _____ discoveries in recent years was found off the coast of Israel. This tiny nation is one of the _____ places per capita on the face of the earth. This makes Israel the center of _____ from surrounding nations.

4. When this coalition approaches, Christians will _____ to others that this war was foretold in the Bible. As this legion comes against _____ _____, God is going to shake the earth with an earthquake. God will bring the _____ _____ together with Israel to fight the coalition.

5. Israel destroyed the nations that came against them in the _____ _____ _____ in 1967. God was with them and He will be with them in the war that is yet to come. Many people will _____ and turn back to Him when they see that _____ ___ _____.

6. This battle involving the _____ _____ is supernatural. God draws _____ against this coalition with torrential rains and earthquakes. Five-sixths of the _____ armies will die in this battle fought on the mountains of Israel.

7. After this war, the world will experience a _____ collapse with commodity prices going through the roof. The earth will be in _____ as it tries to rebuild the _____ but Israel will be a very good position.

8. The _____ can be rebuilt in Jerusalem at the close of this war which would lay the foundation for the _____ _____ to begin for the Jews. Once this occurs, the stage will be for _____ and the abomination of desolation.

DON'T GET THIS WRONG! 113

9. Great tribulation and the Ezekiel 38 War are not events that we can pray away because _____ _____ says they will take place. So, we must be prepared _____ to endure these events and place our _____ in God.

10. Abundant faith is necessary to _____ the severity of these events because if we are here on earth during this time, we will be called to _____ great faith and trust in God. This is not a time for Christians to fear. We know our God is _____ and His army will _____ evil.

11. We are to encourage one another and align our hearts with God in order to _____ with Him during these events. We are not to be _____ by what is going on around us. Instead, we are to be prepared, _____ and _____ for the return of the Lord.

KEY WORDS:

(a) Diplomacy   (b) Coalition   (c) Fortify   (d) Armaments   (e) Anarchy

_____ Alliance of distinct parties, persons or states for joint action.

_____ Weaponry and defense equipment used in military resistance.

_____ Conducting relations between nations; making treaties and trade agreements.

_____ Protect or strengthen against attack; surround with military defense works.

_____ Social disorder due to the absence of governmental control; disobedience; confusion.

SESSION ANSWERS:

1. Ezekiel, dry bones, live
2. borders, coalition, motivation
3. natural gas, wealthiest, antagonism
4. preach, God's nation, Anglo Nations
5. Six Day War, repent, God is God
6. whole world, nature, opposing
7. financial, disarray, economy
8. Temple, sacrificial system, Antichrist
9. God's Word, spiritually, trust
10. endure, demonstrate, victorious, overcome
11. work, overtaken, alert, ready

KEY WORD ANSWERS:

b, d, a, c, e

PERSONAL DEVOTION – DAY 1

THE NEXT PROPHETIC EVENT

READ: EZEKIEL 37:1-10;21-22 // EZEKIEL 38:1-7

These chapters in Ezekiel are miracle chapters. We witnessed one of the prophecies in the last century. It was the prophecy about the coming together of Israel as a nation.

In Ezekiel 37, it was prophesied several years in advance that Israel would become a nation again. This prophecy is often referred to as; The Prophecy of Dry Bones.

I think sometimes we under estimate the miraculous event of Israel becoming a nation again.

After two thousand years these people were dispersed around the world, and all during that time, they had evil empires like Russia and Germany trying to kill and destroy them. What a miracle that they stayed together!

The rebirth of Israel happened on May 14, 1948, and then, in 1967 Israel took back the city of Jerusalem.

In the next chapter of Ezekiel there is an end time war. It is a war that has not happened yet. In the reading it refers to many ancient countries. Let me break down who-is-who in present day sovereign nations.

Gog is the leader of Magog and I want you to picture him as an end time leader. Today, Magog is the nation of Russia and the chief prince of Meshech is Moscow.

Tubal is a city in Russia. Also, when you breakdown the ancient Hebrew, the word *Rosh* or *the prince of Rosh*, is Russia. So, it is the end times leader of Russia that is being spoken about here in Ezekiel.

Today, Persia is Iran. It was just a little over one hundred years ago that the nation of Persia was changed to Iran.

Ethiopia is the Sudan in Northern Africa, and Libya is self explanatory, because we all know where Libya is today.

Gomer or Gomerland is the old Soviet States that surround the Soviet Union.

Togarmah is Turkey and in the original language there is a word *Hich* and most think this refers to Syria while others believe it is just north of Syria.

Put all of them together and Ezekiel 38 refers to the nations of; Russia, Iran, Northern Africa, Sudan, the Old Soviet States, and Turkey. The Bible tells us that God will force them to come down to Israel. Like a fish with a hook in its mouth, He will draw them into the land.

PERSONAL DEVOTION – DAY 2

WEALTH IS THE MOTIVATION

READ: EZEKIEL 38:7-17

In the reading today, the Bible speaks of Israel becoming a nation. We see that there is a great army of people coming to Israel. Its leader is Gog, and Magog is the nation of Russia.

Isn't it amazing that we can read the newspaper today and see this coalition already being put together! Even though we are moving in that direction; it does not mean it will happen next week.

In Ezekiel 38:9-12, we see the motivation for the armies to attack Israel is; wealth.

Let me point out that one of the largest natural gas finds in the history of mankind was just recently discovered in Israel and this has only happened in the last few years. Israel is geographically located in a very strategic point, because when you look at all of the nations in the Mediterranean, plus Northern Africa, Asia and India, you understand that Israel is the focus point of all of those worlds coming together.

The blessing that is upon this little nation is amazing!

The land itself is not that big and it is not that populated, yet, it is one of the wealthiest places per capita on the face of the earth. However, there are nations that surround them that are thousands of years old and they have not obtained the level of society that Israel has in such a short amount of time.

In Ezekiel 38:13, we see some sort of diplomacy taking place. They are asking this coalition group; "What are you doing? Are you coming to take a spoil?"

Those asking the questions are the nations that defend Israel in the end times. Sheba and Dedan is the Saudi Peninsula. Tarshish is England. The young lions are; England, Australia, New Zealand, Canada and the United States of America – the Anglo Nations.

Ezekiel prophesied this event over 2,000 years ago, and we are watching it begin to take place on our television sets every night. This is an exciting time, because once this war is fought, the stage for Antichrist will be set and we will be on the verge of our Saviors return!

PERSONAL DEVOTION – DAY 3

THE EARTH WILL BE SHAKEN

READ: EZEKIEL 38:17-23 // EZEKIEL 39:1-16

Today, Gog the land of Magog, Meshech and Tubal, Russia, Persia, Ethiopia, Libya, and Togarmah are amassing themselves together. Sheba, Dedan, and the Saudi Peninsula, and the merchants of Tarshish, and the young lions, who are the Anglo Nations, are saying to the coalition; "Why are you doing this? Why are you coming down?"

God says, that when this coalition is getting ready to come, we are going to be able to preach to others that this war was prophesied by the Prophets thousands of years ago. And, as this coalition comes forth God is going to shake the earth with an earthquake.

He is going to bring His mountains which are His nations, (the Anglo Nations along with Israel), against the coalition.

God is going to work with Israel. There is going to be torrential rains and a great earthquake which means weaponry and mass destruction.

In Ezekiel 39:1-2, God says, He is against the leader of Russia and this whole hoard of an army. Only one-sixth of this coalition is going to survive. Five-sixths of their armies are going to be destroyed. In Verse 2, we see a very important term; *the mountains of Israel.*

In Ezekiel 39:3-10, we understand this means that whatever the hoard of armies try to do, their strategies will be thwarted.

Verse 9, closes with the time period of seven-years, does this sound familiar? Well, for seven years Israel will be accumulating all of the armaments and the weapons. This includes all of the steel and structures that this hoard of armies brought to the battlefield.

We see a second wave of the great battle in Ezekiel 39:11-16. This war is super-natural and even nature works against the coalition as they come and try to take over Israel.

The Bible tells us that men of continual employment will bury the dead.

Again, this major war is still yet to happen, but when it does happen we will be able to point to Scripture and prophecy and say, "Our God is the God of Israel. The true God. Turn to Him. He is all-knowing and all-powerful."

PERSONAL DEVOTION – DAY 4

ANTICHRIST BREAKS COVENANT

READ: REVELATION 12:7-14

In Revelation 12:13, the dragon, Satan, persecutes the woman which brought forth the man child. Israel is referred to as the woman and the man child is Jesus.

Once the war of Ezekiel 38 happens, the entire world will experience financial collapse and an economic depression much worse than the world has ever seen before. All of this will be in part because of this world war.

We will probably have commodity prices, along with oil and gas prices, go through the roof and the world will be in disarray.

At the end of this war, Israel is in a much different position than it was before the war.

My opinion is; this war sets the stage for financial, political and spiritual Antichrist.

Remember the covenant that Antichrist signs with Israel? It allows Israel to go back to the sacrificial system. In the middle of this time period Antichrist breaks the covenant.

Now, stop and think for a moment, could Israel build a Temple right now and go back to the sacrificial system on the site where the Muslim Dome of the Rock sits? No, it is virtually impossible without starting a third world war themselves.

At the end of the Six Day War in 1967, Moshe Dayan the leader of the Israeli defense forces, allowed the Muslims back on the Temple Mount even though Israel had taken over the whole territory.

I can guarantee you, this would not happen again! After this war, Israel is going to build their Temple and they are going to go back to the sacrificial system.

You see, Antichrist is revealed at the three and a half year mark but the structure of the kingdom that he will rule is set up way before he gets into place.

The platform for Antichrist is being set up now and I believe that when you study this war, the entire world will come together and they will start to set global boundaries that will eliminate those that are not tolerant of one another. Setting extremists on either side.

PERSONAL DEVOTION – DAY 5

IN OUR LIFETIME

READ: EZEKIEL 37:1-10; 21-22

In the last days, extremism of all kinds will not be tolerated. This includes radical Muslims and Christians alike.

Society will get rid of the extremes. Even today, it is becoming illegal in many countries to do what we have the freedom to do in the United States of America. Now, whether the foundation of the extremists is *evil* or *love*; it will not matter because their point of view will be non-tolerant. It is the "non-tolerant" point of view that will not be accepted.

I believe this way of thinking will intensify after the war of Ezekiel 38. I also believe the world leaders will put a global contract in place that will set the stage for Antichrist.

When will this war happen? My opinion is; it will certainly happen in my lifetime because it is already taking shape today in the news. But it could take years before the war begins.

I do not believe there is a long dispensation of time between the end of this war and before we go into the tribulation period. At this point, the stage will be set for the system of Antichrist.

It's only a matter of time before we see the beginning stages of this war.

The threat of all this will cause anxiety around the world, but we know the final result is that five-sixths of their armies are going to be destroyed. After that carnage, I believe we move into the next phase and this will be putting the complete structure together. Whether it happens within a year or two after this war or whether it is five or ten years later, the structure is set.

This war is going to be the next major prophetic happening in the earth.

Think about the excitement! Yes, it is a war, but think about this day whether it's a year or ten years from now, you will remember back when you heard and studied this teaching because the Word of God tells us others will see that this was taught before.

Throughout this series I want to leave you with a strong sense of encouragement!

I want to leave you being prepared, alert and ready for the return of Jesus Christ! This is not a time to be fearful! This is a time to work with the plan that God had designed from the very beginning of time!